Bibliotherapy for Bereaved Children

of related interest

Talking With Children and Young People About Death and Dying
A Workbook
Mary Turner, illustrated by Bob Thomas
ISBN 1 85302 563 1

Finding a Way Through When Someone Close has Died
What it Feels Like and What You Can Do to Help Yourself
A Workbook by Young People for Young People
Pat Mood and Lesley Whitaker
ISBN 1 85302 920

Helping Children to Manage Loss
Positive Strategies for Renewal and Growth
Brenda Mallon
ISBN 1 85302 605 0

Interventions with Bereaved Children
Edited by Susan C. Smith and Sister Margaret Pennells
ISBN 1 85302 285 3

The Forgotten Mourners, Second Edition
Guidelines for Working With Bereaved Children
Susan C. Smith
ISBN 1 85302 758 8

Children, Bereavement and Trauma
Nurturing Resilience
Paul Barnard, Ian Morland and Julie Nagy
ISBN 1 85302 785 5

Good Grief 1, Second Edition
Exploring Feelings, Loss and Death with Under Elevens
Barbara Ward and Associates
ISBN 1 85302 324 8

Grief in Children
A Handbook for Adults
Atle Dyregrov
ISBN 1 85302 113 X

Medical Art Therapy with Children
Edited by Cathy Malchiodi
ISBN 1 85302 677 8

Bibliotherapy for Bereaved Children
Healing Reading

Eileen H. Jones

Jessica Kingsley Publishers
London and Philadelphia

The right of Eileen H. Jones to be identified as author of this work has been asserted by her in accordance with the Copyright, Designs and Patents Act 1988.

First published in the United Kingdom in 2001 by
Jessica Kingsley Publishers Ltd,
116 Pentonville Road, London
N1 9JB, England
and
325 Chestnut Street,
Philadelphia PA 19106, USA.

www.jkp.com

Library of Congress Cataloging in Publication Data
A CIP catalog record for this book is available from the Library of Congress

British Library Cataloguing in Publication Data
A CIP catalogue record for this book is available from the British Library

ISBN 1 84310 004 5

Printed and Bound in Great Britain by
Athenaeum Press, Gateshead, Tyne and Wear

Contents

Acknowledgements

I wish to extend my thanks to all who encouraged and helped me to modify my original thesis to produce this book.

Looking for people in differing caring professions concerned with children and bereavement, I have been fortunate to obtain advice from the Revd Canon Sydney Thomas, Dr Keith Greenlaw, psychotherapist, and David Lee, a former social services team manager. Thanks too to Roger Craddock, whose expertise produced the explanatory figures for Chapter 6. Also to Mr Malcolm Hopkins of Carmarthen Library who guided my quest for children's books.

I am most grateful to three authors, Nina Bawden, Sue Mayfield and Joan Aiken, who so readily replied at length to my enquiries concerning the inclusion of death in their children's stories.

I am indebted to Curtis Brown Ltd for permission to make a critical review of the book *Squib* by Nina Bawden; also to the Royal College of Medicine for permission to quote from the May 1999 Journal.

This book would not be possible without the continuing help and support of the children and parents, who have to be nameless, but who gave so readily of their time in reading and discussion over the five years of the study.

My thanks too to the many people in diverse caring professions who gave up their time to talk to me, to forward their opinions, to write to me and to send extracts of articles and tapes.

Introduction

Estimates indicate that in Britain 200,000 children under the age of sixteen have experienced the death of a parent or carer, approximately 18,000 a year. In 12,000 cases the father has died, in 6,000 cases, the mother or other female carer, three quarters through accidents. (Figures from Cruse Bereavement Care 1999.) Many other children have suffered bereavement through the deaths of siblings.

Generally, children are remarkably buoyant in the face of bereavement. They do not appear to need to work through a process of stages in grieving as adults do. Children of seven and under do not understand the finality of death and most older children and early teenagers cope adequately provided they are within a stable, loving environment and are included, if they wish, in the family funeral arrangements and mourning rituals. Youngsters in their later teens, particularly boys, tend to find adjustment more difficult. At that age they are aware of the implications of family restructuring, don't want to be seen crying, bottle up emotions and fail to release tension, which may result in unexpected behaviour. Unresolved childhood grief can manifest itself in emotional or behavioural social problems years after the bereavement. Intervention programmes such as counselling may be recommended for children with difficulties. In the past 15 years the number of children's bereavement programmes has escalated. But can that be the answer? I agree with Dr R. Harrington (1999) in the title of his article in the *Journal of The Royal Society of Medicine* – 'Counselling bereaved children may do more harm than good.' Harrington argues that in structured programmes the counsellor may well introduce suggestions that could prove harmful. His research shows no convincing correlation between childhood bereavement and delinquency or mental health problems in later life.

Nevertheless there are many children, albeit a small proportion of those bereaved, who do need help in coping with bereavement.

Occasionally, when counselling has proved too direct an approach for children who find it difficult to talk face to face, I have introduced ordinary but carefully chosen children's novels concerning the topic of death. Counselling in this way can be flexible, either completely non-directive or leading to a productive dialogue.

Many parents have questioned whether children do grieve, trying to understand how recently bereaved youngsters listen to pop songs, sing, laugh and play games in an apparently normal mood. Children can appear to switch their sad moments on and off. But they may need to be allowed to grieve in their own way, sharing with others if that is their wish. It's natural to shield a child from sadness, but this may well impede the grieving process.

Unresolved early childhood grief can have profound adverse effects through adolescence, lasting well into adulthood. Some surveys have suggested that people bereaved as children are five times more likely to turn to crime, dependency on drugs or to need psychiatric help later on in life. Other longitudinal studies completely refute that claim (Harrington 1999).

There are children who need help – we should not dismiss or underestimate the effect which bereavement can have on children. Let us look at just four of those children:

Janine, 10 years old, sobbed uncontrollably at her mother's funeral. In the church her father struggled to disentangle her hands from the coffin handles. As the coffin was lowered she sat down and dangled her legs over the grave. Her distraught relatives, longing to comfort her, were rebuffed. Eventually she was carried away screaming, much to the distress of her six-year old brother who re-lived the scene in nightmares.

Six months later Janine's teacher expressed concern about the child's preoccupation in school, both in and out of lesson time, little attention being paid to approaches from teachers or peers. Formerly a chatty child, Janine now seldom spoke, except each morning to whisper a request to her class teacher that she might remain indoors during break and lunch time. Ignoring her friends' persuasive tactics, often staring at them with an unsmiling blank expression, Janine seemed to be in a world of her own. Her paternal grandmother, who had moved in to care for the family after the funeral, was concerned about Janine's lethargy and her poor appetite, resulting in a noticeable loss of weight.

Jamie, aged 12, attending his father's funeral, sat at the back of the crematorium chapel, away from relatives, apparently engrossed in his electronic game, ignoring adults' approaches. Later, seemingly oblivious to others, he sauntered to the burial site, refusing requests to assist in burying the ashes, remaining stubbornly aloof.

Two months later in school, Jamie became aggressive towards his peers, fighting being his main communication with them. He contradicted his teachers and was frequently reported for disruptive behaviour in the classroom. At home his mother had to endure bouts of rebellious behaviour and profuse swearing. Outings to public places were impossible for fear of criticism of his bizarre behaviour. She felt unable to care for him at home and enquired about him being taken into care for a while.

Fifteen-year-old Peter, on his return from school, had found his mother lying unconscious on the bedroom carpet, dressed in her outdoor clothes, clutching her handbag. Through his training as a St John's first-aider Peter knew that his mother was beyond help but he called the ambulance before alerting his father at work. Throughout the funeral and afterwards people remarked favourably on Peter's composure. Within a few weeks he threw himself wholeheartedly into his school work, giving up the sports at which he had previously excelled and declining to meet or go out with his friends, pleading for time to study.

Jonathan was eight when his grandmother died suddenly at her home, a pub in the adjoining village. His grandparents had always made a great fuss of him, in fact he had been quite spoilt by them, staying overnight at the pub several times a week. Jonathan was considered too young to

attend the funeral and was sent to stay with an auntie with whom he had
had little previous contact. After Granny died Grandad could not cope
with Jonathan staying at the pub. Jonathan took this to heart, assuming
that he wasn't loved any more. He refused to visit the pub, misbehaved
at home, defying his parents and stealing money from his mother's
purse, using it to buy chocolate, crisps and biscuits which he stashed in
his desk at school and at home in his wardrobe.

Jonathan became the classroom clown, easily distracted and re-
sponding to any cue for misbehaviour. His rapid weight gain led to
referral to a dietician. The disruptive behaviour continued for three
years, resulting in referral to the Schools Psychological Service for
placement at a special unit for behaviour modification prior to his
moving up to comprehensive school.

In these four children we see but a few different reactions to bereavement. Janine's behaviour evoked deep sympathy and kindness, Jamie's
attitude disgust and condemnation. Peter's behaviour, although
changed, was admired. Jonathan was excluded from primary school on
grounds of disruptive behaviour, causing his family much embarrassment.

Each child showed signs typical of unresolved grief. We saw outward
excessive expression of grief followed by withdrawal, loss of appetite
and excessive eating, initial apparent indifference, expressions of
extreme anger even against people outside the family, rudeness,
swearing, physical violence, intense interest in one aspect of life to the
exclusion of others, appearing to cope well with grief and behaving
normally, also stealing and attracting attention by odd behaviour.

Janine, Jamie and Jonathan were referred to the Schools Psychological Service on grounds of abnormal behaviour. Peter was referred to
Cruse Bereavement Care for counselling. That's when I met each one of
them.

None appeared to respond to approaches through direct counselling.
Janine didn't want to talk, '...because it makes me cry'. Jamie responded
with verbal aggression and rudeness. Peter was polite, willing to talk
about generalities in his life but when asked about family matters immediately clamming up. Jonathan appeared not to care about his behaviour,

remarking on one occasion, 'I like behaving like I do, it's fun and it makes others laugh, so I'll carry on'.

The families of Janine, Jonathan and Jamie had expressed concern about their child's habit of retreating to another room, playing loud music, watching videos and playing computer games rather than taking part in normal family activities. 'Not natural' was the general opinion. In the few weeks prior to meeting Peter I had read two children's novels with themes of death and bereavement, one telling of a boy who had found his mother dead on his return from school (*The Charlie Barber Treatment*, Carole Lloyd 1987). After four counselling sessions with Peter I tentatively offered that book to him, informing him of the theme but neither elaborating on the story nor giving any expectation of his response.

Three weeks later he returned the book, asking if he could talk about the main boy character. 'I've bought a copy of the book because I wanted to mark some of the happenings which were like me. I've read those over and over again,' he told me, 'and somehow I feel released, from what I don't know, but I do. Dad won't talk about Mum but I want to. I felt in the book that I was following and watching how that boy coped. His friend listened to him. I felt I wanted to join in the conversation. The author couldn't have written like that if she hadn't experienced those feelings some time.' He volunteered the fact that he had cried about the fictitious characters and events. 'Not about Mum, directly, but for the characters. Maybe that's what released me.'

Talking about the book proved, over six months, to be the turning point in Peter's progress through his journey of grief. He was curious about the reason an author might choose to write about death and how many more similar books were in print.

Many questions began to arise in my mind. Could children's fiction be used in bibliotherapy for these and other bereaved children? (Bibliotherapy can be defined as the use of books and stories as part of the treatment of emotionally and mentally disturbed people.) To what extent and depth might a novel's plot delve into the effects of bereavement? Would children identify with the characters? Could reading about fictitious characters help children to examine their own unexpressed feelings, personally and privately or to parent, peers or therapist? Would such books prove too morbid?

Such questions led to discussion with others involved in the care of bereaved children: psychologists, social workers, teachers, staff of police child protection units, children's home staff and also parents.

Further aspects were highlighted that might need to be addressed if a study was to be made:

- Was there published research evidence supporting the use of bibliotherapy, particularly through existing children's fiction?

- How many children's fiction books with the topic of death were available?

- Were there enough published books which included the topic of death to suit a wide range of situations and ages?

- Did school or public libraries stock such books?

- How could one identify appropriate books?

- How did an author communicate with a child reader, particularly on such a delicate subject?

- Since an emotionally disturbed youngster tends to have a poor concentration span, what form of writing could capture and maintain a child's interest?

- How should books be chosen for a child with a particular problem?

- How could selected books be introduced to the child: in the classroom, in discussion with parent or other family member, in private reading or recommended by a counsellor?

- Would it be feasible, or even of value, to recruit children, both bereaved and non-bereaved, to read and comment on selected books?

So many unanswered questions indicated the probable worth of a pilot research project into the use of children's fiction books in therapy – bibliotherapy in bereavement.

Certain areas for investigation were identified:

- To carry out an overview of the research literature in support or otherwise of using children's literature in bibliotherapy; to identify a particular mode of bibliotherapy for which children's fiction could be of value. (Chapter 1)

- To locate support for the rationale of the use of death topics in children's fiction. (Chapter 2)

- To review the variations in the representation of death in children's fiction from the late-nineteenth century to the early-twenty-first century and to validate the use of appropriate literature. (Chapter 3)

- To study the nature of children's reading and identify suitable narrative presentations. (Chapter 4)

- To identify a selection of children's books with a topic of death and to review them, not only by their content, but also by means of a critical literary assessment. (Chapter 5)

- To devise a suitably accessible classification for this chosen list. (Chapter 5)

- To identify any 'fictionalised fact' books, specifically written for bereaved children.

- To select one item of children's fiction for a deeper analysis of its specific suitability for bereaved children. (Chapter 6)

- To recruit child readers (both bereaved and non-bereaved) to provide first-hand opinions of the selected book. (Chapter 6)

- To identify, with the children's help, any specific needs a bereaved child might have when selecting a suitable book. (Chapter 6)

- To evaluate the results of the research and trial, considering the implications. (Chapter 7)

The aim throughout the study was to collect and collate information and facts from various sources, providing a compendium of information that I believed would prove valuable and relevant to the many people in different walks of life who care for bereaved children.

However, one must beware of being too simplistic. There are many complex issues involved in helping children through what could be a sensitive journey through grief. Mourning is a process which cannot be hurried. The length of time cannot be specified, each person being an individual in his or her response and reaction to bereavement. Nevertheless, it is hoped that this study will highlight bibliotherapy through fiction as another approach which smooths that journey through grief, particularly for children, possibly for adults too.

CHAPTER I

What is bibliotherapy?

What is bibliotherapy?

Bibliotherapy is the practice of using books and stories as part of the treatment of emotionally and mentally disturbed people. This mode of treatment is not a recent innovative introduction. Cohen (1987) in 'Bibliotherapy: Using literature to help children deal with difficult problems' claims that the word *bibliotherapy* was coined as far back as 1916 by Samuel Crothers from the Greek words for book and healing, or service (biblion/book, therapeia/service).

Riordan and Wilson (1989) inform us that bibliotherapy, under other names, is at least as old as the sign over the entrance to an ancient Greek library that proclaimed it as 'the healing place of the soul'. Various alternative terms have been used for this form of therapy: library therapeutics; bibliocounselling; literatherapy; reading therapy; therapeutic reading; biblioprophylaxis.

Whilst these definitions indicate a general agreement on the nature of bibliotherapy, subtle variations in approach and focus are worthy of notice.

Howie in Clarke and Bostle (1988) gives his definition as: **guidance towards the solution of personal problems through directed reading**.

Berg, Devlin and Gedaly-Duff (1980) define bibliotherapy as: **a process of using literature to help children express themselves in order to promote healthy adaptation**.

Jalongo (1983) quotes definitions given by three other practitioners:

from Overstad (1981): **using books to promote mental health**;

from Weinstein (1977): **using books to resolve personal problems**;

from Garner (1976): **a process of dynamic interaction between the personality of the reader and the literature**.

This last definition is not specific to bibliotherapy as it reflects the model of reading defined by several literary critics such as:

Cresswell in Blishen (ed) (1975): **a private dialogue between one writer and one reader**.

Other definitions or descriptions relevant to both bibliotherapy and reading include Wall (1991) who refers to: **a transaction between writer and reader**.

Crago (in Hunt 1990) refers to **a child–book interaction**.

I add here three items of relevance to bibliotherapy from Lesnik-Oberstein's (1994) list of statements which form the basis of educational literary criticism:

- Literature can help children to understand feelings.

- Children can identify with book characters who experience similar feelings.

- Literature can help children to become sensitive to the feelings of others. (Statements 8, 9, 10. p.109.)

The above extracts suggest that bibliotherapy has been used with children but its value as an agent of change is not universally proved. The use of fiction, as opposed to factual or self-help purpose-written books in bibliotherapy remains essentially unvalidated, research showing a range of results from a general ineffectiveness to positively successful improvement. From a perusal of ClinPSYC and Medline databases it is evident that bibliotherapy for children has been used extensively in the USA from the late 1960s, addressing specific themes of anxiety, including bereavement. In 1989 Riordan and Wilson (op.cit.) reported a growing interest in bibliotherapy, noting that up to 86 per cent of psychologists used self-help books in therapy and counselling. (They do not indicate whether these books were fiction or non-fiction.)

Lenkowsky (1987) notes the expansion of bibliotherapy during the period of two decades prior to his writing, but highlights the need for controlled research to prove or disprove the efficacy of the therapy. He does, however, admit that as a preventive against adverse effects on children experiencing change in their lives, including death, bibliotherapy has been found effective as part of a larger treatment plan.

The fundamental belief of all bibliotherapists is that through a structured or guided approach using selected books focused on specific needs, reading can influence a child's thinking and behaviour, leading to, in this context, a successful outcome from the trauma of bereavement.

At the time of writing, primary care groups within the Calderdale and Kirklees Health Authority (Huddersfield) are supporting a bibliotherapy pilot scheme run by the library services. Liaising with GP surgeries, the aim is to promote the idea of therapeutic reading as an alternative to drugs, leading towards improved mental and physical health. This new scheme is targeted at adults in the first instance. I would strongly support its eventual extension to children.

Brown (1975) places bibliotherapy in two distinct categories, as a **science** or as an **art**. Practised as a **science** it would involve psychiatrists and psychologists generally using a psycho-analytical approach in a one-to-one situation, delving to find who the child 'is'. In this context Lesnik-Oberstein (1994) refers several times to the 'psycho-analytical' child who with the psychologist or psychiatrist will build a mutual construct based on what the child might or might not reveal to the therapist, creating an external interpretative dialogue and narrative. Essentially this is a positively **directive** interaction but could lead to a need or recommendation for reference to books. Those books chosen would probably be purpose-written for bereaved children.

Non-medical therapists, whether specifically trained or not, may well practise bibliotherapy as an art. It is this approach which is the focus of the search for suitable children's literature within this discussion.

Using bibliotherapy as an **art** a therapist offers or makes available carefully selected published narratives. The child, through reading, has the freedom to hold an internal dialogue in accordance with his unique life experience, initiated by the author's narrative. As in any personal reading the child has the opportunity to 'discuss' his problems internally and may, as a result, wish to engage in dialogue with the therapist.

The vital issue here is the choice of book. With a suitable presentation of topic and level of readability the therapist hopes and expects that the child will be led in the first place to clarify his own personal thoughts, position and interaction in his own immediate environment, then possibly to extend this to a wider situation.

As a child reads or, in the case of a young child, listens, he senses a common bond with the story's characters. If or when he notes that the characters have problems to be solved he shares vicariously in the character's dilemma. If recognised and deemed relevant to the child this could lead to a reflection on his own personal circumstances and he may even adopt some of the characters' coping strategies as his own. How far the child will allow himself to become immersed in the characters and events rests with him. He does not necessarily need to identify with the characters, he may prefer to read merely as an onlooker but still internalise the emotions in the story and process his own plans for positive change.

Essentially, as an art, bibliotherapy is **nondirective**, in that it is the child's choice to extract from the narrative what he finds relevant to his emotions, without any initial overt direction from the therapist. Nevertheless, it may be of therapeutic value to project discussion on to characters and events. That would be at the discretion of the youngster, resting, probably, on the rapport between child and therapist.

Opportunity for discussion should always be available if a child wishes to enter into the verbalisation of emotions or to outline possible solutions. However, the therapist would be wise to heed the warning given by Cullinan and Rosenblatt (Cullinan and Golda 1981) that a child's free response to a novel may be 'drowned out' by teachers (or therapists) who persistently analyse and question responses. Crago (in Hunt 1990) also observes that a child's initial perception may change if asked to comment on the book, plot and characters in question.

Mention must be made of **counselling**, which differs from either of the previous approaches, being basically a dialogue approach in which the counsellor guides the child in unravelling his thoughts and actions.

Who or what is a bibliotherapist?

His/her prime role is to 'prescribe' books, based on an interpretation of a client's needs. Skills and accessible facilities include:

- an appreciation of children's fiction
- a knowledge of how children read fiction
- an understanding of children's emotions
- liaison with schools and public libraries
- access to databases
- liaison with schools medical staff, Schools Psychological Service, health centres, hospices and charities concerned with child welfare
- organisation of parent, teacher or child groups to discuss suitable books.

A bibliotherapist is concerned with the most suitable choice of books based on an author's presentation of death and relevance to a child's particular situation. In this context the main goals of bibliotherapy as an **art** that directs the choice of books are:

- to assist children in recognising that emotions can be expressed in text from which they may extract information
- to help them to understand the concept of death
- to help them cope with the death of a person close to them
- to provide information on problems
- to provide insight into problems
- to present new values and attitudes
- to promote an awareness that others have dealt with the same problems and have come to terms with them or overcome them
- to outline possible solutions.

The search for suitable books calls for a selection that is freely available through booksellers, in school and public libraries.

Berg *et al.* (1980) in *Bibliotherapy with Children Experiencing Loss* claim to exclude the use of books intended for educational and recreative purposes. They do not substantiate their claim. No doubt they would reject all of the fiction books which I have found in practice to be therapeutic.

I would argue that if parents and teachers are preparing a child for life, this should not preclude any relevant book. Cullinan and Golda (1981, p.39) echo this. In their opinion: 'The experiences we have during our lives shape and are shaped by the books that are important to us.'

Many children's novels, though not written specifically for therapeutic purposes, are suitable for bibliotherapy. Practice has shown that books suitable for bibliotherapy are or can be intrinsically and inextricably bound up with 'normal' everyday reading and when chosen as such would not be seen by a bereaved child to be personally targeted.

The selection of suitable books rests not only on subject matter but on a critical assessment of the text. Teachers are aware of the effect of reading on children, and bibliotherapy practised as an art could be within the province of most teachers of literature, children's librarians and school counsellors. However, Jalongo (1983), who is a firm believer in using fiction in therapy, warns, 'Teachers might question the extent of their role in providing bibliotherapeutic experiences for independent readers who are usually responsible for their own book choices' (p.798).

Her consideration that the same strategies needed in the preparation of successful lessons in general are applicable to bibliotherapy in particular leads her to suggest that teachers are certainly at an advantage in helping emotionally disturbed children by using selected classroom books.

A British educational psychologist, Evans (1971), joins the controversy, arguing that a teacher's role is not as therapist. In a journal concerned with children's literature he criticises another contributor, Tod, whose writing on the treatment of childhood stress calls for clarification as to whether one is looking at the bibliotherapy issue or looking at how childhood stress is dealt with in children's fiction used in schools. He warns that in choosing a suitable book for bibliotherapy it is imperative to see the **child** first in the situation rather than see the **situation** first. He advises caution in making decisions, diagnoses and choices from the flimsiest of evidence. Nevertheless, Evans confirms the value of using children's literature for distressed children, remarking that there is '...no doubt at all that the power of the novelist can help us to understand and acquire new insights into problems of children under stress and to use these to help us to deal more sensitively and imaginatively with children in our care' (p.50).

Parents who have read some of the novels reviewed in Chapter 5 confirm Jalongo's (1983) opinion, remarking on the empathetic sensitivity of authors dealing with deeply emotive topics concerning terminal illness and death, embracing aspects which some parents and teachers prefer to evade in discussion with children.

Positive and productive results further depend on the therapist having a thorough knowledge of the concept of 'the reading child' in general (an extended discussion of this aspect is found in chapter 4). Attention to the individual child together with the content and presentation of the topic of death in the book is vital. Brown (1975) summarises the main concern in the application of bibliotherapy. Referring to the required essential and extensive knowledge of both child and book, he states, 'We need more than the right book for the right person at the right time' (p.334).

Morris-Jones in Clarke and Bostle (1988) deplores the lack of identified appropriate literature for bibliotherapy use but acknowledges the increasing interest in 'this effective therapeutic tool' (p.44) reporting:

> At a local level in Dyfed (Carmarthenshire) in 1987 consultation developed with the library service in an attempt to organise access to any literature resources. The key to the direct reading programme however was what the response of individuals within the library was to this and the notions of bibliotherapy very much underpinned those developments. (p.45)

Although Morris-Jones was concerned with children on probation her general remarks (above) could equally relate to bereaved children. In my own liaison with the Carmarthenshire Library Service I have found an increasing interest in bibliotherapy, particularly by one librarian, previously a bereavement counsellor, who has now compiled a selection of suitable fiction books to help emotionally disturbed children, including the bereaved. This would suggest that there is a distinct role for the children's section of public libraries to liaise with professionals working in the sphere of childhood anxiety, to provide for bibliotherapy. A specialist children's librarian not only has an extensive knowledge of published books but also an insight into children's reading habits. Although bibliotherapy aims to promote insight and enlightenment, as a technique it has certain variables that could become limiting factors:

- Over-expectation: the reader may believe that merely reading a piece of literature will resolve a problem, whereas, in reality, the purpose of the reading is simply to put in motion the thinking and coping behaviour that will finally work through to a solution.

- The reader may acquire more problems through identifying with a strong or appealing character, particularly in a first person narrator situation from which the child may have difficulty in distancing himself.

- A reader may find imaginative literature too stimulating, which could impede the resolution of problems.

- Some teenagers may tend to rationalise their problems when reading about them, rather than gaining insight into them.

Bibliotherapy may be said to be prescriptive, not predictive. We can prescribe a book for a particular child but no one can predict how that child really feels about a bereavement or how he will respond to the book's contents. Evans (1971) suggests it might be better to use stories as a method of getting to **know** a child's problems rather than as a means of **treating** him.

Suggested approaches to introducing selected books include:

- book used as a class reader in school when there can be a general discussion of contents

- book included with others in a limited choice

- child given a specific book to read privately

- child given a book with follow-up discussion.

Introducing a class reader or presenting a book in a limited selection is entirely non-directive and not obviously targeted in the first instance at any bereaved child. Nevertheless the teacher may choose to inform a bereaved child privately of the nature and intensity of the emotional content of the book.

Bearing in mind the possible impact on a sensitive child, the selection of recommended books reviewed in Chapter 5 has been graded according to the strength of emotional content:

- **mild** – not likely to cause distress

- **mod**(erate) – may cause some emotional upset

- **emo**(tional) – containing some graphically emotional scenes that could provoke considerable distress.

An experienced bibliotherapist or teacher would know instinctively whether to recommend a book directly related to a particular problem or whether to casually suggest recreational reading within a chosen collection of books. Any reader will experience 'reverberation' when he 'listens' to the come-back or resonance that the text arouses. This leads to an active dialogue between himself and the 'other' person in the text. The teacher or therapist who makes the choice of a book can implicitly navigate the child through their emotional problems. This avoids pressure on the child to verbalise or reveal their own emotions, as discussion is based on the characters' problems. With the addition of inevitable subliminal learning when messages embodied in the text are absorbed without the reader's awareness, the reader can be far more relaxed and less defensive and secretive than with a psychologist's direct approach. Children need time to internalise any parallel emotions and insight found through identification in a story and then need to distance themselves from the issues both in the text and in themselves in order to have a more objective view of their situation. The very fact that a book can be read again and again, probably revealing deeper meanings in the text on successive readings, can hasten this process.

I consider that these aspects support the notion that a selection of children's fiction novels, as opposed to purpose-written books, can make a valuable contribution in helping a bereaved child through his grieving process.

Bibliotherapy is no panacea or 'cure-all'. Success or failure may depend on certain critical factors to be discussed in the following chapters:

- Chapter 4 discusses the identification of 'the child' as a reader, how an author addresses a child to establish a relationship between author and reader, consideration of how the bereaved child might differ from other children in his reading. Reference is made to the list of desirable factors compiled by six bereaved children aged 10 to 14.

- Chapter 5 refers to a system of classification and critical analysis of books dealing with death.

- Chapter 6 takes one book, **Squib** (Bawden 1980), to make an analysis of its success features, intended as a guide towards the selection of books specifically for bereaved children, who tend to have limited concentration spans.

CHAPTER 2

How real do we want
our realism about death?

On the eve of the Booker Prize Awards in July 1997 BBC2 hosted a discussion on the merits or otherwise of exposing children to contemporary, intensely realistic fiction including the topics of sex, drugs and death. Opinions were divided. Rosemary Sandberg, a literary critic, considered that since children know life is not all happiness they need true-to-life fiction to support and rationalise their thoughts. She cited Judy Blume as one author who was not afraid to write for children on controversial topics. (Blume wrote *Tiger Eyes*, a particularly emotive story of teenage anguish and rebellion, see Chapter 5, p.75.) John Andrews, General Secretary of the Professional Association of Teachers, agreed with Anne Fine, a children's author, that children should have access to reality in fiction and have the freedom to form their own opinions.

However, Fred Inglis, echoing objections from the older generation, regretted the loss of innocence, regarding extreme realism in books as conducive to widespread cynicism. It is refreshing to note that children's opinions, recorded for the programme, presented a point of view that they should not be wrapped in cotton-wool and they wanted to read what other children were experiencing. One child looked upon intense sadness and fear as essential in order for others to be aware, to understand and offer help.

Discussion on this topic continued on BBC1 on the morning of 15 July with Leslie Sim, a member of the Carnegie Committee, voicing his opinion that too much of modern children's fiction was sordid. This was echoed by Nick Seaton of the Campaign for Real Education who did not like to see children growing up too quickly by reading about sex, death and drugs.

I would argue that it is the children's opinions that are the most valuable. Although we need to respect parental attitudes, we have to ask 'how real do we want our realism?' That is the crux of the matter if we are going to use children's fiction with true-to-life situations for bibliotherapy.

Much controversy exists over the presentation of realism in books. Marshall (1982) in *An Introduction to the World of Children's Books* comments on the marked increase in the production of children's books with social realism, including death, as the main content, both in the genre of the teenage novel and also for younger children. She says, 'Real life in books is a form of education and of bibliotherapy' (p.78).

Since in this study the search is for books containing social, or in the term which Hunt (1994) uses, domestic realism, how then do we define realism? 'An interesting concept,' remarks Hunt who sees realism sitting uncomfortably between fantasy (in which he see the rules of the world being suspended) and romance (where the rules are bent). He offers several definitions and explanations of realism, such as: 'books in which the laws of the ordinary world are not suspended (to take the broadest possible definition of realism)' (p.167). He adds, 'There is, as I have suggested, a strong British school of what might be called "domestic realism" – realism restricted to what the child might see and comprehend but which does not duck the implications of what is seen' (p.171).

Further he approves, '...reality and realism, presenting the probable or actual actions of recognisable beings in recognisable circumstances...' (p.184) and '...the "new realism", a genre which has developed steadfastly towards dealing with serious (and often brutal) social problems' (p.147).

Finally he remarks, 'A lot of recent books that deal with realism deal with some very hard aspects of the world indeed, from the horrific including child abuse and mass destruction to the taboo such as sex and death' (p.167).

Townsend (1965) describes realism in children's books as fiction in which described events are such as might happen in real life, not necessarily in contemporary life. This remark is applicable to Joan Aiken's books, *Black Hearts in Battersea* (1965) and *Dido and Pa* (1986), both written in Dickensian style and set in the fictitious reign of James III – both books are reviewed in Chapter 5.

Does Marshall (1982) reach the essence of realism in her remark: 'So realism is not always a blow-by-blow description of everyday reality involved in factual and situation realism: it is also the presence of factors with which the reader can identify emotionally, those that cause the reader to think, "that's how I feel", and which are real to him' (p.76).

Can one concur with Hunt's (1994) comment that there is general disagreement over which topics may be appropriate, attractive, relevant or even comprehensible to a child, and that 'the water is likely to be muddied by taboos, notably of sex and death' (p.16)? Both *The Boy in the Bubble* (Strachan 1993), reprinted four times in 1994 and again in the following two years, and *Falling Apart* (Wilson 1989), reprinted four times, feature death and sex as major issues, but issues which are presented sensitively and realistically.

Hunt's (1994) reference to the taboo of death echoes that of Westall (1978) who views death in children's books as rather an extreme taboo, remarking, '...you don't have to go as far as death to find taboos in the children's book world' (p.42).

Long before Hunt's declaration there are opinions that would argue against this notion. Eyre in Haviland (1973) identifies two parallel genres in children's literature reflected in popular demand by children: one of folk tales and fantasy and the other of social realism, pointing out '...there are critics, librarians, teachers and writers preaching the need for ever-increasing social realism' (p.337). Eyre commented on the need for writers at that time to be concerned with intellectual, emotional, moral and social problems. Similar issues form the basis of criteria for book choices in Carmarthen Children's Library. (Source – recent discussion with children's librarian.)

Many authors of popular children's books have traversed these taboos in such aspects of realism, although this has not been given credit by some literary critics. But Trease (in Blishen 1973) remarks, '...the taboos of a generation ago are gone' (p.23).

The majority of books selected for this study were written post–1970 and indicate a distinct change in attitude towards the inclusion of death. Topics of death range from the main themes of illness, dying, death and grieving, as in Little's (1984) book, *Mama's Going to Buy You a Mockingbird*, to the mere mention of death as a minor part of a story as in the majority of novels by Joan Aiken. She announced in Fox (1976) that '...I also try to introduce the fact of death in my stories' (p.56). In a personal letter to me she explained that after the death of a very close relative her children constantly asked for stories with realistic happenings in them.

Jalongo (1983), commenting on the dearth of children's fiction books suitable for emotional problem bibliotherapy, remarks, '...divorce, death and sexuality tend to be highly controversial, even among adults' (p.16). In my experience of counselling it has appeared to be partly because of this adult attitude that many children need special help in resolving their grief problems. I firmly believe that fiction can play a positive role in this area. Grieving children may appear outwardly unaffected by bereavement and, having no outlet in conversation with adults, may express their anxiety through aberrant, atypical behaviour, which is often interpreted as sheer naughtiness. I trust that when some indication of this aspect is woven into contemporary children's fiction where fictitious but believable characters are 'seen' to behave in similar ways, 'heard' to express similar feelings and 'allowed' to mourn, grieving children will understand that their own feelings are normal.

To believe that children's literature could and even should include these so-called taboo subjects is not such a recent idea. After many years of 'nice' stories with little realistic emotional content, critics began to voice opinions towards a change to realism. Catherine Storr in Tucker (1978) wrote, 'I believe that children should be allowed to feel fear...and to meet terror, pity and evil' (p.146).

I find forward-looking support for the use of realistic children's fiction in bibliotherapy from Heins, writing in *Children and Literature*, (Haviland 1973) quoting from Edward Fenton's *Horn Book* (1968):

As for all the other problems related to life, including death, it is impossible to overestimate the capacity of children to feel, suffer, understand and share them all if properly presented. But they must be in terms of action and plot. (p.409)

I consider this last sentence to be the nucleus and strength in the choice of bibliotherapeutic books. No matter how comprehensive the story content concerning death, the book has to be judged a 'good book' in literary terms.

CHAPTER 3

How do authors present death?
Then and now. The late nineteenth century to the early twenty-first century

Children's libraries, both school and public, report a steady interest in classics such as *What Katy Did*, *Little Women* and *Oliver Twist*. Although written a hundred or so years ago and set in a vastly different lifestyle such stories still appear to appeal to children.

Surprisingly there are some marked similarities between the presentation of death in children's literature during the late nineteenth century and the latter half of the twentieth century, with, in between, a distinct change of direction. In the late nineteenth and early twentieth century domestic novels for children and adults reflected life at a time when death was a frequent experience in many families. With an infant mortality rate of 142 per 1000 live births and only 4 per cent of people living beyond 65 years in 1900, most children must have witnessed death at close quarters. Compare this with 1999 UK statistics of an infant mortality rate of 5.87 per 1000 births and a life expectancy of 77.37 years. (International Database, US Census Bureau)

Avery (1968), writing the preface to a revised edition of *Froggy's Little Brother* (afterwards referred to as *Froggy*) notes that the author, 'Brenda' (Mrs Castle Smith), originally at the time of writing (1875) used *Froggy* as a vehicle of a propaganda campaign to highlight the abject poverty and misery of the poorest people in London. She aimed to awaken the sympathy of children to the plight of the desperately poor and homeless urchins of the streets of London, known as 'street arabs'. In the 1968 edition Avery has edited out several passages that were totally out of date, bearing little or no relevance to life today, together with the original concluding paragraphs asking readers to send money to the Ragged Schools and children's charity homes.

In a similar vein Dickens, in his preface to *Oliver Twist* (1837), said that he '...wished to show, in little Oliver, the principle of Good surviving through every adverse circumstance, and triumphing at last...'

Both authors highlighted, through the characters of Froggy and Noah Claypole, the benefit of being given the opportunity to become a charity child, when a trade could be learned to support a family, rather than remaining a workhouse child.

In books of that era a certain mystique appeared to surround an orphaned, displaced protagonist (main character) such as Sara in *The Little Princess* (Burnett 1905), Mary in *The Secret Garden* (Burnett 1911) and the child protagonist in *Heidi* (Spyri 1880).

Graphic descriptions of dying, early infant death and grief in literature reflected contemporary reality and would presumably at that time have been generally accepted by child readers. Typhus, cholera and consumption were rife and together with extreme poverty and malnutrition caused many deaths. In *Jane Eyre* (Brontë 1847), we read of Helen Burns dying of consumption. *Oliver Twist* (Dickens 1837) tells of the nurse attending Oliver's birth having had thirteen children of whom only two survived. Dickens' description of Oliver's mother's weakness at the time of his birth suggests malnutrition, the cause of death of many real workhouse children who were weak and undernourished from babyhood.

At that time Christian morality was at the forefront, reflected in various nineteenth-century novels. Even the penniless child character Froggy refused a chance to earn money through pickpocketing, declaring that he would rather starve than steal. In the preface to the 24th edition (1889) of *Eric, or Little by Little*, Farrar declares the book to be '...written with one single object, the vivid inculcation of inward purity and moral purpose.'

That this approach was socially acceptable to many readers appears to be well borne out by the fact that within forty-five years there had been thirty-six editions of the book. Whilst Darton (1982) acknowledges this success, he remarks, 'Nearly everything that can be said against maudlin sentimentalism, against sincere and pious self-delusion has been said about this astonishing book' (p.286).

Farrar's religious persuasion is frequently and overtly presented throughout the book, such as when the boy Russell (Eric's friend) is preparing for his own death. He utters prayers and blessings for the friends he leaves behind and on his deathbed the reader learns that '...the gentle holy pure spirit of Edwin Russell had passed into the presence of its Saviour and its God' (p.170).

Oliver, on the night before Fagin's hanging, begs Fagin to pray, 'Upon your knees, with me' (*Oliver Twist*, p.276).

Fictional child characters appear to reflect children's strong faith in God during this period. The character Benny in *Froggy* prays to God to keep his pet house-mouse from death by the cat. Froggy's mother is said to be 'God's gift to the toilers of this world...for she had loved God's Holy Sabbath' (p.17).

Eliza (in *Jane Eyre*) is described as '...in matters of religion, a strict formalist...went to church thrice on Sundays and as often on week-days as there were prayers' (p.201).

In *What Katy Did* (Coolidge 1865) Katy's mother, who had died when Katy was twelve, is said to have been, '...but a sad, sweet name, spoken on Sundays, and at prayer times' (p.11). At Beth's death in *Good Wives* (Alcott 1869), the reader is informed that '...father and mother guided her tenderly through the Valley of the Shadows and gave her up to God' (p.225).

From the 1920s onwards children's books reflected life in a world where mortality rates had decreased, fewer children died and life expectancy was extended. Children's literature at this time reflected the changing attitudes towards children in which adults, through their efforts to preserve childhood as an essentially happy period of life, tended to protect children from pain and suffering. They were shielded from overt sadness and grief and seldom attended funerals. Towards the middle of the twentieth century the trend in children's fiction was to move away from the domestic scene. Within the school story genre, particularly in the sixty-two somewhat 'Utopian' *Chalet School* series, death was seldom mentioned except perhaps when it might serve to highlight a protagonist's character, such as the 'orphan syndrome' of Eustacia in *Eustacia Goes to the Chalet School* (Brent-Dyer 1929). Her mother died of pneumonia and we read that, 'Eustacia mourned properly' (p.5), whatever that might mean to a child reader. The account of the child's father's death of a heart attack is baldly stated: 'His head was on the desk. He had been dead some hours, and it was obvious that death had come painlessly' (p.8). Bereft of parents, Eustacia changes her behaviour and becomes arrogant and objectionable, particularly towards those of lower social status. This was a common theme in stories at the time, reminiscent of Mary in *The Secret Garden*. Child characters were given increasing independence and provided with greater freedom to engage in adventures of their own making. They were unencumbered by adults who were often of little consequence except as undesirable or interfering characters, as in Enid Blyton's *The Famous Five* and *The Adventure* series. In these and her romanticised far-fetched stories of school life, the *St Clare's* and *Malory Towers* series, all published in the 1940s and 1950s, death is seldom mentioned.

However, a noticeable change has become apparent since that time, notably during the period of the 1970s to the 1990s. Once again death has featured in children's books, even as the main theme in *Mama's Going to Buy You a Mockingbird* (Little 1984, afterwards referred to as *Mockingbird*), or as a secondary theme in *Fox in Winter* (Branfield 1980), in some instances described in as graphic detail as in nineteenth-century books.

Children's books published since the 1960s show little of the directly targeted Christian morality and pious sentimentalism of the late nineteenth century. Not that religious connotations are totally absent. The child narrator in *A Taste of Blackberries* (Smith 1975) remarks, '…it was hard to think about God when something as small as a bee could kill your best friend' (p.85).

In *I Carried You on Eagles' Wings* (Mayfield 1990) the teenager Tony, in despair facing his mother's death, sobs in his anguish, 'What sort of God is there? What sort of God lets people die of horrible diseases? What God at all?' (p.118)

In answer to a child character's question about the nature of heaven the newly bereaved mother in *Mockingbird* reads out a passage from Revelation: 21 verse 4. 'Death shall be no more and never again shall there be sorrow or crying or pain. For all these former things are past and gone.' (p.132)

In *Emma Says Goodbye* (Nystrom 1990), Emma remembers her aunt as being '...tall and tanned and strong – and dancing round Jesus' (p.43).

In some respects the present-day approach mirrors that of the latter half of the nineteenth century in that death, now being an accepted part of 'life', can once again be openly depicted in real-life stories.

To compare and contrast the presentation of death in books from the earlier (late nineteenth century) and later (late twentieth century) eras I use the following aspects:

- declaration of expected death

- moment of death

- announcement of death

- immediate reaction of persons experiencing an actual death

- expressions of relief at release from suffering

- the effects of long-term unresolved grief in children.

Declaration of expected death

Several late-nineteenth and early-twentieth-century novels presented the dying person announcing his/her own impending demise. In *Uncle Tom's Cabin* (Stowe 1852) Eva announces, 'I'm going to leave you. In a few weeks, you will see me no more.' (1961 edition, p.289)

Beth in *Good Wives* (Alcott 1869) tells her sister, 'I have a feeling that it was never intended that I should live long...' (p.170), and later expresses it metaphorically, 'I think the tide will go out easily' (p.172).

In a similar vein, Helen, in *Jane Eyre* (Brontë 1847) suggests that Jane has come to bid her farewell. '"Are you going somewhere?" asks Jane. "Yes, to my long home – my last home."' (1976 edition, p.67)

In contrast, authors of books published in the 1980s and 1990s tend to present the announcement of impending or actual death in dialogue, frequently by a third person reporting to another family member, as in a parent addressing their child. '"I don't know if this is the right thing or

not...we thought you ought to know...He is not going to get well.'"
(*Mockingbird*, p.82)

In *Eagles' Wings* (Mayfield 1990) Tony asks, "'Mum's going to die, isn't she?" "Yes," he [Tony's father] said expressionlessly.' (p.119) Again, in *Two Weeks with the Queen* (Gleitzman 1995), the protagonist Colin is told directly of his brother's impending death, first by his mother, "'Luke's going to die...'" (p.35), and second by an eminent cancer specialist in a London hospital, "'He's not one of the lucky ones. He will die.'" (p.92)

Even in the anthropomorphic world of *Badger's Parting Gifts* (Varley 1984) Badger personally forecasts his own impending death, telling his friends that he will be '...going down the Long Tunnel before long.' (Opening 3).

Moment of death

In both eras the focus tends to be on quietness as the dying person takes his or her last breath. In *Froggy* we are told, '...and then with a little sigh and the faintest sob the mother's soul passed over to the eternal shores' (p.123). As Benny (Froggy's brother) lies dying we read, 'A look of unspeakable rest and satisfaction settled on his features...he remembered it in his mother's face after she was dead' (1968 edition, p.149).

Similarly, in *Good Wives*, '...and in the dark hour before the dawn, on the bosom where she had drawn her first breath, she quietly drew her last' (quotation from Penguin edition, 1965, p.151). Describing Edwin Russell's death in *Eric*, Farrar writes, 'He sighed very gently; there was a slight sound in his throat, and he was dead' (p.169).

In a more modern description from *Eagles' Wings* (Mayfield 1990, p.136) '...she stopped breathing. They all sat, frozen, waiting for another rasp... There was an aching silence.' From *See Ya, Simon* (Hill 1992, p.120) as Simon, age 14, lay dying from muscular dystrophy '...very peaceful. He just stopped breathing.' In *Emma's Cat Dies*, again there is a peaceful end, 'Emma saw her aunt search for one last breath – then stop' (Snell 1984, p.34).

Authors appear to accord these peaceful deaths only to 'good' characters. In sharp contrast and well in context with an evil and loathsome character in Joan Aiken's story, *Dido and Pa* (1986), set in Dickensian style, is a particularly gruesome description of death:

> And before their aghast eyes the Margrave began to shrink, to shrivel and dwindle, the lips pulled back from the teeth, the jaw fell open, the eyes glazed and filmed; with the final rattling gasp, which sounded like a wild ironic cackle, the patient writhed from head to foot and lay lifeless on his bed. (p.246)

The author makes sure that little sympathy is evoked for this character at his moment of death and indeed a child reader may well relish such a well-deserved horrific ending.

Announcement of death

The tendency in modern books is to present the plain blunt fact that someone has died. In *Seeing in Moonlight* (Matthews 1995), "'I'm afraid I've got some terrible news...Mikki was knocked over and killed tonight...'" (p.106). In *Mockingbird*, Jeremy is told, "'Your father's dead, Adrian's dead'" (p.108). Similarly, in *Bridge to Terabithia* (Paterson 1977), Jess's sister tells him, "'Your girl friend's dead...'" (p.115).

There does not appear to be any instance of such direct informants in nineteenth-century books so far mentioned.

Immediate reaction of persons experiencing an actual death

There is a close resemblance of behaviour between reactions recorded in nineteenth-century and present-day books. The reaction to Eva's announcement, in *Uncle Tom's Cabin*, is, 'Here the child was interrupted by bursts of groans, sobs and lamentations' (1982 edition, p.289). Eric's reaction to his brother's death is, "'O, Vernon, my own darling brother! O God, then he is dead!" And, unable to endure the blow, he fainted away' (p.302).

A more gentle reaction is seen in *Good Wives*, 'With tears and prayers and gentle hands, mother and sisters made her ready for the long sleep...' (p.112).

Froggy's immediate reaction to his brother's death is particularly touching: "'Oh, Benny! Benny, come back! I can't live without you, Benny! Benny!' Then covering the little dead body with frantic kisses, he sobbed.' (*Froggy*, p.151)

Paterson, in *Bridge to Terabithia*, describes Jess's protestations of disbelief and denial: "'No!' Jess was yelling now. "I don't believe you. You're lying to me'" (p.117), and similarly in this extract from *Blackberries*, 'Some awful instinct was hammering on my brain. I tried not to listen. "Jamie is dead, darling," she said.' (p.46)

In *Eagles' Wings*, just after the actual death description, there is a particularly emotive account of the father's and son's reactions:

> Tony felt numb. He couldn't speak…His dad bent forward and placed his face on his wife's arm. His eyes were clenched shut, his face twisted up with pain…'Alison,' he said softly, as he kissed her arm, 'Alison…' It shocked Tony to hear him speak her name with such tenderness…His dad was crumpled by the bedside, doubled up as though in terrible pain and howling like a baby…Part of him [Tony] wanted to run from the room – to be alone – but he couldn't take his eyes off this shaking, helpless figure that was his father. His father opened his hand and enfolded Tony's fingers in his. He gripped them in wild desperation, crushing them tightly as he sobbed into the bedclothes. (p.131)

This scene is all the more poignant as the reader has already been informed that, as the vicar's son, Tony had always seen his father as a tower of strength to other people in bereavement situations.

In *Emma's Cat Dies* (Snell 1984) we read that, 'Her family held each other and cried' (p.43). Newman (1995) in *Steve* tells us that Gemma 'cried, shouted, yelled and stamped in disbelief on hearing that her father had died'.

Expressions of relief at release from suffering

This is common throughout both nineteenth and late-twentieth-century children's novels. Alcott describes 'a face full of painless peace…' (*Good Wives*, p.225) and from the same page, '…the beautiful serenity that soon replaced the pathetic patience that had wrung their hearts so long…' In *Mockingbird* the children's mother tries to comfort them, '"The doctor said it was a blessing"' (p.109). Tony (in *Eagles' Wings*) is shocked and angry when he overhears his father telling someone that they had decided to let things take their course as it was the kindest thing to do.

Related to the effects of long-term unresolved grief in children

I have not found any references to the more bizarre effects of this aspect in late-nineteenth-century children's books. It could be argued that this reflects society's acceptance of openly expressed grief at that time, but it may also underline the lack of psychological knowledge of grief reactions in children.

Recognition and a deeper understanding of unresolved childhood grief appear in children's fiction of the 1970s to the 1990s. In the opening chapter of *Falling Apart* (Wilson 1989), Tina, aged fifteen, is preparing to take an overdose of drugs. She decides she can no longer live with the guilt over her twin brother's death at the age of eight, although seven years have passed. Another instance of morbidly prolonged grieving through guilt is highlighted in *Memory* (Mahy 1995) in which Jonny is haunted by the death of his sister five years ago. We are told that, '…before falling asleep these questions had haunted him for a second or two, allowing them to be glimpsed, but never grappled with' (p.2).

Some of Kate's problems in *Squib* (Bawden 1980, see Chapter 6), can be attributed to long term mourning coupled with guilt.

Certain expressed emotions, feelings and examples of motivational fervour appear to be equally relevant to either of the periods considered above. As an example I take *Froggy*, published 120 years before *Two Weeks With The Queen* (Gleitzman 1995). Apart from the time difference and social setting there is a striking similarity between these two books, the main theme and events running in close parallel, as indicated in Figure 3.1 (p.47). In *Two Weeks With The Queen* the storyline is brought up to date by the inclusion of air travel, the child having travelled by himself from Australia to stay with his aunt in London, his parents hoping to save him from the trauma of seeing his younger brother die.

That there is a dual meaning in the title (which also brings the story to a contemporary level) only becomes apparent towards the end of the book. Bringing in the alternative meaning of 'Queen', the boy is befriended by a young gay man whose close friend dies of AIDS in the same hospital where the child finally understands that his brother will surely die.

	Froggy	Queen
year of publication	1875	1995
time scale of story – few months	yes	yes
boy protagonist	yes	yes
younger brother ill	yes	yes
brother – terminal illness	yes	yes
home/income	poverty	adequate
parents	dead	alive
setting	London	London
brother's quest for cure	yes	yes
child on his own quest	yes	yes
Queen involved	yes	yes
tries to see Queen	yes	yes
sentries bar his way	yes	yes
writes letter to Queen	yes	yes
tries to contact doctors	yes	yes
rebuffed many times	yes	yes
visits hospital	yes	yes
anger at privileged society	yes	yes
outcome – brother dies	yes	yes

Figure 3.1

These extracts have hinted at some of the close similarities and contrasts between late-nineteenth and late-twentieth-century presentations of the emotions and feelings common to bereaved children. Chapter 5 expands on some of these aspects, identifying and analysing certain presentations in modern children's novels that may be particularly relevant for bibliotherapeutic purposes.

CHAPTER 4

How do writers
and readers communicate?

Since the purpose of this study is to identify children's literature suitable
for specific readers – bereaved children – I propose to pursue the
questions of the identity and relationship of writer and reader,
narrational orientation, the reading child and any specific aspects concerning the bereaved child reader.

The writer addressing the child reader

All successful writers are good communicators. Obviously what they
write appeals to their readers, yet as Chambers, A. (1979) in 'The
Reader in the Book' remarks, '…I am not suggesting that as an author
writes, he necessarily has in front of his mind a particular reader' (p.65).

This raises several questions. What might be the authorial intention?
Is there an imagined intended audience or is there some other motivational cue for writing a story?

The research literature reveals that many writers have pondered
these questions. A wide selection of motivational cues have been cited
by authors. Roald Dahl and Joan Aiken claim that they originally wrote
for their own children, some of their stories satisfying a family need
such as bereavement. Other authors state that they write in the light of
their own childishness but not about their own childhood. Nina
Bawden, in Blishen (1975) *The Thorny Paradise*, explains: 'I write not as
a grown-up looking back, but as a former child remembering the
emotional landscape I once moved in, how I felt, what concerned me,
what I wanted to know' (p.62).

In Fox, (1976) *Writers, Critics and Children*, Bawden, referring to her first children's novel, tells us, 'I just became eleven years old again' (p.7).

Garner, in Chambers (1980) *The Signal Approach to Children's Books*, is adamant that he does not write *for* children, but for the '…child that I once was' (p.310). He agrees with Chambers that the act of putting pen to paper is an act of wishing to speak to someone, wishing to communicate and claims that he feels a sense of urgency to share an excitement which he doesn't really understand himself.

Astrid Lindgren, quoted in Lesnik-Oberstein *Children's Literature* (1994) also affirms that she does not write books for other children, but for the child she once was, adding, 'I write about the child I am myself. I write about things that are dear to me…just to please myself' (p.75). Catherine Storr, in Blishen (1975), speaking of her successful *Marianne* series, considers herself fortunate that her books sell well since she wasn't writing any of her books just for any child but for herself. She speaks of the urgency to write '…I write what I need to write, not what someone else needs…it can't be the first consideration' (p.29). Ransome is of the same opinion, writing in Chambers, 'You write not *for* children, but for yourself and if by good fortune children enjoy what you enjoy, why, you are a writer of children's books' (p.257).

John Gordon, in Blishen (1975), disagrees with those authors who claim that they write only for themselves. He thinks they are deluding themselves. In his opinion, '…the instant pen touches paper there are other eyes looking over my shoulder' (p.35).

Helen Cresswell, who terms her inventive and eventful stories such as *The Signposters* (1988) 'explorations', claims, 'I do not make a habit of thinking why I write for children…I do not know where I am going until I arrive there' (Blishen (1975), p.109).

Most of this selection of authors' remarks concerning their motivation to write children's books does not suggest that there is a child reader in the author's mind at the time of writing. However, in response to children's comments, sometimes an author does revise a plot. As Joan Aiken told me in a private letter, 'I had intended the death of Dido in my book *Black Hearts in Battersea* (1965) to be permanent, but I had such a strong protest from a child reader that I had to reverse the decision.'

Whatever the motivational origin of a successful children's story the line of communication between writer and reader is far from direct.

The diagram below represents Wall's adaptation of Chatman's diagram (Wall (1991) *The Narrator's Voice,* p.4). It illustrates the flow or process of communication between writer and reader within six sections.

Real author	Implied author	Narrator	Narratee	Implied reader	Real reader

Figure 4.1

The two real people at the ends of the communication continuum seldom, if ever, chance to meet. Five of these sections can be identified with some degree of accuracy. The 'implied reader' appears to be an indistinct, variable and flexible concept synthesised by critics in trying to imagine for whom the book was written.

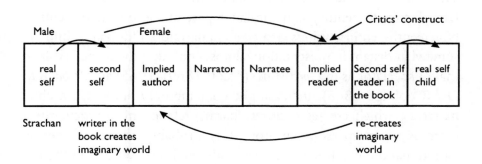

Figure 4.2

If we take Strachan's (1993) book *The Boy in the Bubble,* together with the comments of five teenage readers, it will be seen that the above diagram can be expanded to eight sections.

When Ian Strachan, the real author who lives in his real family-life world, creates a story he becomes a 'second self', the first stage in the communication flow. Considering the inclusion of many personal and intimate references to a female adolescent's physical and emotional development this 'second self' suggests a female author. Five teenage readers of this story, two boys, three girls, each independently built up an impression of a female author and questioned whether the name Ian Strachan is a pseudonym. (It is not.) In the minds of these readers the implied author 'who' is seen by the reader to be the 'person' behind the narrator in the text became virtually tangible, suggesting that the implied author, though obviously not a person, cannot be depersonalised. An implied author is a variable concept since as each child interacts with the text he will interpret the story and form his own concept. In this story the real-life male author becomes the female implied author, who in turn becomes the source and voice of the first-person fifteen-year-old girl narrator. Through the text this narrator addresses the narratee who becomes the reader-in-the-story who is free to assume whichever gender he or she chooses.

Narrational orientation

There has been a noticeable change in narrational address between the late nineteenth century and the latter part of the twentieth century. Nineteenth-century writers created adult narrators addressing children, somewhat distant in presentation, almost confining the reader's role to that of spectator as in *Good Wives* (Alcott 1869) (1965) and *What Katy Did* (Coolidge 1865). Increasingly, contemporary authors use child narrators, which creates a closer sharing relationship particularly if there is a first-person narrator. It is probably these changes in narrational presentation which has made the books written in the late twentieth century more suitable for bibliotherapeutic use. A child is addressing a child.

In *The Boy in the Bubble* (Strachan 1993) the fifteen-year-old girl narrator vividly and sensitively tells the story of her love for a boy who lives in a sterile tent. A twelve-year-old boy, whose name is not revealed in the story, narrates *A Taste of Blackberries* (Smith 1975). Both narrators address child narratees at a peer-level relationship, narrowing but not eliminating the barrier between narrator and narratee. The choice of a child narrator obviously limits the extent of language and given information to that of a child of commensurate age.

Garner, in Chambers (1980), sees a narrator as a third entity, created from the mind of an author and almost a character, apart from the author's 'other self'. Several child readers have remarked on this even when narration was not in the first person (see Chapter 6 concerning the book *Squib*).

Children respond differently to narrators' varying roles. In *Your Friend Rebecca* (Hoy 1981), the child **narrator/protagonist** tells her own story, communicating directly with the narratee to create a close confiding relationship. '…I've never felt so sorry for myself in my life as I do just now, so you'll have to excuse me; I'm sorry' (p.73). The whole story is told as if the reader is alongside the narrator and of a similar age. With this form of narrator–narratee relationship the reader would probably remain as 'listener' rather than identifying with the character. Where the main protagonist tells the story as a narrator/focaliser the focus of character and focus of narrator are woven into one.

In *Little Nym* (*A Creepy Company*, Aiken 1993), the gardener tells his own story in an appealing avuncular style from **the role of a minor character** who is part observer and part participant. Another variation is the **first-person narrator/observer** as in *My Disability* (in *A Creepy Company*) in which the adult narrator occasionally directly addresses the narratee, '…Have you ever eaten fish, my dear? Don't start.' (p.31)

A **third-person narrator/observer** but not a character is used in *Goodbye, Chicken Little* (Byars 1979), where the narrator merely describes the characters and events and therefore cannot reach into the depths of feelings and thoughts.

An **omniscient** (all-knowing) **third-person narrator** who not only relates details of characters and events but also goes deeply into the nature and thoughts of the characters is to be found in *Squib* (see Chapter 6, p.116). It was probably because of this deep insight that several child readers perceived the narrator in *Squib* as a **participant**, but not an identifiable character in the story (see summary of readers' comments in Chapter 6, p.110).

In *We, The Haunted* (Johnson 1989) there are two first-person narrators. The teenage girl, Caro, who opens and closes the story, narrates five out of twelve chapters in the **present tense**, not obviously directed at the narratee, more musing over the situation to herself and 'allowing' the narratee to overhear. The other narrator, the girl's friend, tells his story in the **past tense**, commenting on the situation as if he had heard all that had been said in the other chapters. The two narrators complement each other in story content, taking chunks of the story in turn and covering two or three chapters each.

An astonishing **eleven characters** narrate the story in *Shadow Man* (Grant 1996). Jennie, the main character, as girlfriend of a boy killed in a car accident, narrates ten out of forty-three chapters. The dead boy himself covers seven chapters (written in letters addressed to his teacher), the undertaker's son of the same peer group narrates four chapters, the dead boy's brother five chapters, the teacher four chapters and three chapters each from the man who attended the accident, the dead boy's father and his other brother. An uncle narrates two chapters, the sheriff and a friend one each. All these character narrators are focusing on the bereavement situation, but because that focalisation oscillates between their own actions, feelings, observations and other peripheral characters, the story tends to become fragmented and hard to follow. Some readers found it difficult to switch from one narrator to another, causing two (out of six) adolescent readers to abandon their reading of the book.

Providing **both adult and adolescent character/narrators** enables the author to present more varied and wider angles of reaction to life events which enrich a story – provided the reader can co-ordinate the character relationships.

How the narrator addresses the narratee will influence the reader's participation in the story. A reader may respond to a first-person narrator as a **listener**, as an **observer** in parallel with the narrator or may **identify** with the narrator or a character, giving the reader freedom to remain distant or to become involved.

A third-person narrator does not necessarily distance the reader, who may identify closely with a character or situation if the narrator is felt to involve the reader in a situation or experience similar to his own. In *I*

Carried You on Eagles' Wings (Mayfield 1990), the third-person narrator–narratee relationship can become so close that the observer may be drawn into the grieving situation very vividly. Even to some non-bereaved readers, the story proved so emotionally fraught with tension that they could not at the time continue reading (though each one returned to the book to complete the story). I too had to leave the book to 'compose' myself before continuing.

I consider that the change in narrational orientation will prove to be one of the strengths supporting the use of modern children's literature in bibliotherapy.

The reading child

Text is inanimate and therefore can only be brought to 'life' through the reader's response. To what depth that text can prove meaningful rests on the effect that text has on the reader. Koubovi in 'The Therapeutic Teaching of Literature' (1987) remarks, 'Each work of literature awakens the reader to new, different and unique aspects of inner life' (p.75). It is highly unlikely that any two children will respond to a text in identical ways. The possibilities in response are many, as outlined by Frank Hatt (quoted in Hunt 1991):

> One reader will read different texts in different ways; one text will be read in different ways by different readers. One reader will read the same text differently on different occasions; indeed, he will read different parts of the same text in different ways during the course of one reading act... (p.98)

As will be noted in Chapter 6, bereaved and non-bereaved children read differing meanings into the story *Squib*.

How a child responds to a text is governed to a large extent by certain basic factors, some of which are limiting factors such as cognitive development, language competence, literary competence and ability to read the text fluently enough to make sense of the plot. Other influences on interpretation of the text vary widely according to a child's experiential resource bank, his creative imagery and his ability to visualise settings, characters and events. His psychological resources enable him to identify with characters in their situations and to appreciate varying strata of meaning in the text. Appleyard, in *Becoming a Reader* (1991) points out that 'The story is not the same as the text on the page, nor is it the reader's uniquely personal response to the text' (p.9). Each reader creates his own image from the text creating the story from his personality and history which he brings to the reading. Each reader will elaborate on or shut out what he does not want to acknowledge.

Some children have described their reading experience as 'listening' to the narrator in the text. A ten-year-old girl reading *Squib* (Bawden 1971), felt that someone was talking to her throughout the story. She expressed such a closeness with the narrator in the text that at times she felt the urge to question the narrator or pass comments. To some extent this child appeared to be developing a dialogue between her reading self and the narrator. Using non-directed reading the child is free to read and re-read, to explore attitudes and feelings and even release unexpressed emotional processes which the text evokes. Aiken, in Fox, (1976) *Writers, Critics and Children*, claims to prepare for a book to be read and read again providing something new to offer at each re-reading. She aims to provide '…a sort of graded series of concepts, graspable at each stage of development' (p.20). This is apparent in her six collections of short stories (see Chapter 5, p.64).

Identification refers to the process by which a reader immerses himself into a unique relationship within the text using his experiential resources to bring about a certain compatibility with the writer. No reader will ever synthesise the story to match the writer's creation. Identification is a primarily unconscious activity, spontaneously aroused by reading a literary text. Characters, settings, emotions, happenings and moral opinions may be immediately recognised or held at an unconscious level at first, to be reconstructed later within the child's 'reading life'. How far the child will allow himself to become immersed in characters and events rests with the child, who does not necessarily need a direct identification but may choose, consciously or otherwise, to be merely an onlooker. There is also bound to be a certain amount of subliminal absorption of messages embedded in the text, also retained in the unconscious or processed to conscious level later. An anxious child being unaware of what is happening at subliminal level would therefore be more relaxed than if a message were more overt. We can compare one particularly overt description of a dying scene in *I Carried You on Eagles' Wings* (Mayfield 1990), quoted on page 37, in which little is left to the imagination, descriptions being graphically factual and possibly proving disturbing; whereas in this following extract from *Seeing in Moonlight* (Matthews 1995), emotion expressed by a first-person sixth-form narrator allows for flexibility of time and depth in its interpretation. 'I hadn't realised that it [bereavement] would be like a disabling illness and that I wouldn't be able to carry on as normal, because "normal" has changed.' (p.121)

Generally the closer the similarities between the reader's own thoughts and feelings and those in the text the deeper the identification. Conversely, if a reader, most likely a young adult, discovers differences between his own situation or feelings and those expressed in the book he will probably begin to reassess his own thoughts and rationalise in his identity with the newly presented situation. This 'reverberation' or bouncing-back of ideas, valuable for bereaved readers, is not confined to children.

Hunt (1990) refers to the 'unyielding reader' (p.93), pointing out that children are not mature enough to be able to give themselves up to the story as presented in a book. Many skilled writers do create a successful writer–reader relationship allowing the child to enter into the story to the depth at which he is capable.

The bereaved child reader

Bereaved children's emotions may interfere with their learning, impede their concentration, cause increased irritability and indecisiveness, all of which will affect their reading, their interaction with the text and their interpretation of the story and comprehension skills. I regard Townsend's remarks, in Blishen (1975), as particularly relevant to bereaved youngsters.

> I think that what the reader gets from the book has a very oblique and uncertain relationship to what the author puts in. The reader draws out what he wants and needs and perhaps what he gets is related mainly to what he himself puts in. (p.156)

Considering the aspects discussed in this chapter, eight bereaved youngsters, aged ten to sixteen, were requested to suggest criteria underlining a choice of fiction books that might help them extract as full a support from the content as possible. They asked to work independently in the first instance and then to pool their ideas and opinions to present this composite list of fourteen items:

1. An easy read.

2. A clearly defined story-line, preferably told in sequence of events with few unresolved blanks.

3. A clearly defined setting, preferably concentrated in short passages of richly descriptive language.

4. One first- or third-person narrator throughout the book.

5. Plenty of dialogue rather than long passages of narrative.

6. Five or fewer child protagonists.

7. Stimulating opening sentences to each chapter (to refocus attention).

8. Few, if any, illustrations (prefer to create own images).

9. No 'happy-happy' family situations unless as an outcome of resolving problems.

10. Recognisable instances of the effects of bereavement, both emotional and behavioural.

11. Some 'tear-jerkers' (so that the child has a reason to cry without losing face).

12. Varying depths of strata of information.

13. True-to-life instances of coping strategies in bereavement and forecast of happier times to come (reverberation opportunities).

14. Hardback copy of book (apparently paperbacks have proved to be irritating because they are awkward to hold open when relaxing, most of the children's 'healing' reading taking place in bed).

Some of these criteria rest on the writer's skills in content and presentation. Others, which may well be specific to bereaved children, will be taken into consideration in the selection of recommended books listed and described in the next chapter.

CHAPTER 5

Classification of books

The intention in this study was twofold, first to devise a system of classification providing convenient reference to bereavement aspects in books addressing the topic of death and then to select and review children's novels within the chosen classification system.

Basic classification

Essentially, classification within the context of non-directive bibliotherapy has to provide for flexibility and cross-referencing, therefore rigid classification is impracticable. Possible divisions and subdivisions are numerous, being neither inexhaustible nor fully comprehensive.

Figure 5.1 *Children's Book Classification – Topic of Death* (p.53) indicates a variety of broad categories, subdivided to pinpoint books covering specific facets of the main aspects and topics of death and grief. Figure 5.2 *Children's Fiction Depicting Bereaved Children's Responses in Behavioural and Emotional Styles* (p.54) further analyses one of the broad categories, that of children's responses to bereavement, indicating novels which refer to these specific aspects.

Figure 5.3 *Books for Bereaved Children Matched to Age Groups* (p.55) follows the divisions generally adopted by publishers or suppliers of books. Ideally an elimination key would lead directly to a specifically suitable book, but this is not feasible as one book may well appear under several different categories. Taking *John's Book* (Fuller 1993) as an example, it is listed under three headings: 'death pre-story'; 'parent', and 'accident' in Figure 5.1. It is also listed in Figure 5.2. under five headings: 'mistrust of adults'; 'disbelief'; 'evasion'; 'assuming role of deceased'; and 'anger'. A further look at Figure 5.3. indicates that *John's Book* may provide suitable reading for children within the eleven- to fourteen-year age group.

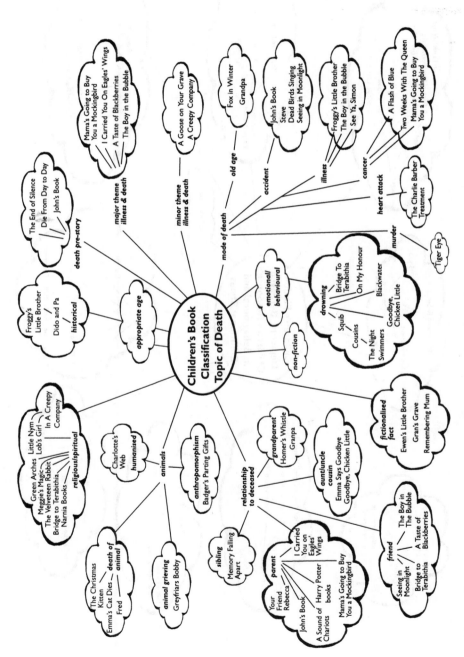

Figure 5.1

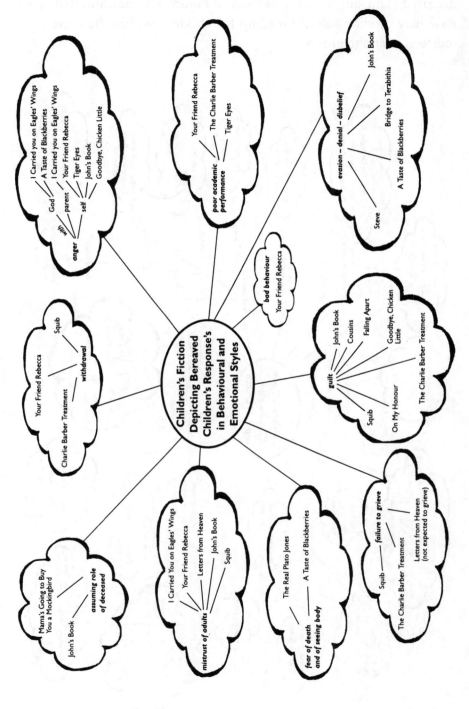

Figure 5.2

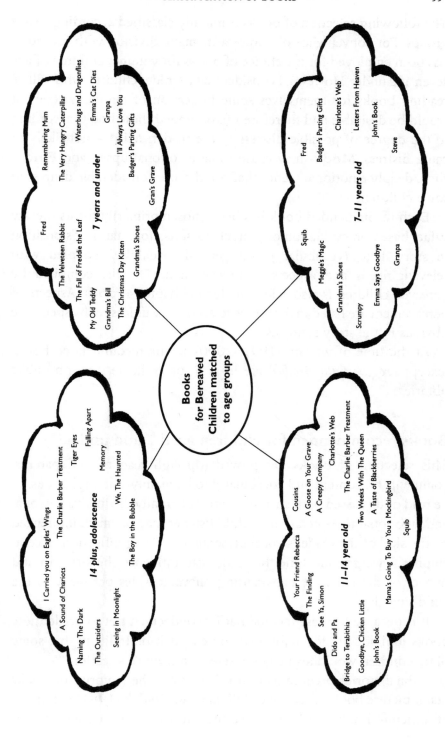

Figure 5.3

The following selection of books is initially classified according to age groups. For convenience of choice a thematic division with footnotes has been employed for the choice of books for younger children of age seven and under. However, I consider that for older children who will be reading books for themselves some indication of emotional content would be desirable and therefore I have graded these books according to the degree of possible distress to the reader: **Mild** – not likely to cause distress; **Mod** – may cause some emotional upset, and **Emo** – some deeply emotional scenes that could cause considerable distress in some children.

Each recommended book has been chosen primarily for its literary value, based on evaluation of plot, characterisation, narrator's position in story, lexis (vocabulary) and general readability, coupled with relevant needs and aspects of bereavement. The list compiled by bereaved children is also acknowledged (Chapter 4, p.50). Aspects of bereavement are listed in footnotes to each story unless such aspects are obvious in the story synopsis.

At the time of writing (1999–2000) all the recommended books (except *Froggy's Little Brother*) are in print or available through public libraries.

Books recommended for children aged 7 and under

This selection of books has proved (through readers' and parents' comments on content and vocabulary) to be mainly 'sharing' books, to be read or discussed with an adult, with potentially distinctive personal and emotional interpretation. A child listener may be much influenced by the skill of the reader's vocal presentation. Using inflection, accent, emphasis, weight and tone the reader can influence the strength and impact of the story, perhaps adding relevant asides pertinent to the child's needs.

It is because of these factors that I have decided not to grade these books individually for emotional content. It is quite likely that some older children would also enjoy a selection from this section.

Animal stories predominate in this section, the majority of books being picture books, if we take Cullinan and Golda's (1981) definition of a picture book that '…the text and the art are woven inseparably together' (p.80). Meaningful messages are clearly presented in the pictures which not only support but in some instances extend and enhance the text. Hans Wilhelm, who wrote and illustrated *I'll Always Love You* (1985) (described later on p.59), provides clear simple watercolour pictures which reflect the text only, without adding any extraneous information. In contrast, *Fred* (Simmonds 1987) uses detailed pictures expanding the storyline far beyond the text and giving scope for discussion on relevant aspects. Most of these books do not have numbered pages – my references are given to an 'opening' (double page spread).

I have grouped these books according to theme and, if appropriate, in alphabetical order of author within that.

ANIMAL STORIES: ANTHROPOMORPHIC

Varley, S. (1984) *Badger's Parting Gifts*

A deeply moving description and explanation of death, grief and recovery is told in this particularly poignant story of Badger's preparation for his impending death and his friends' immediate and later reactions. It is delicately illustrated by the author in anthropomorphic mode reminiscent of Beatrix Potter's style in colour and dress. Badger leaves notes for his friends, settles down and gently rocks himself to sleep, dreaming of running down a tunnel towards a light. The sadness of Badger's friends is described in tear-jerking detail. The animals, still grieving after a few months, find comfort in talking together about Badger. Four animals tell of how Badger helped them to gain a skill, each one of which is recognisable to a child. Eventually the animals are able to smile as they remember Badger's contribution to their lives. A touching ending comes when Mole walks on the hillside where he last saw Badger. He feels he wants to communicate with Badger. 'Thank you Badger,' he says softly, believing that Badger would hear him. 'And...somehow...he did.' (final opening)

Aspects of bereavement:

• talking about the deceased person is acceptable as part of the healing process – children like to believe that a dead person can hear them

- grief is an ongoing process
- grief becomes less painful as time passes
- a bereaved child reader or listener is given 'permission' to cry
- people who have had a near-death experience have described a light seen at the end of a tunnel.

DEATH OF A PET

Dale, E. (1996) *Scrumpy*

When his mongrel dog Scrumpy dies, Ben is inconsolable. He mopes around, refusing even to think about having another dog as there will never be another Scrumpy. Ben avoids visiting any place near where he used to take Scrumpy. Many months later he sees a dog resembling Scrumpy chasing a cat and realises that he is ready to welcome another dog. This story highlights the intensity of grief felt at the death of a pet.

Aspects of bereavement:

- it is common to find children avoiding a place where deceased and survivor shared pleasure together
- children find it difficult to accept a substitute for the deceased
- the death of a pet can be as traumatic as the death of a person.

Herriot, J. (1986) *The Christmas Day Kitten*

A vet narrates the story of Debbie, who befriends a stray cat. On Christmas Day an emaciated cat brings its kitten into the kitchen and then dies on the mat in front of the fire. The kitten survives. The family shed tears over the dead cat and for the orphaned kitten, which settles down happily with three Basset hounds. Two five-year-old children in our reading group rejected this book because of the Victorian-type pictures.

Aspects of bereavement:

- experiencing an actual death
- sharing grief with the family.

Simmonds, P. (1987) *Fred*

A delightful, amusing and comforting book presented in comic format with softly coloured detailed illustrations showing a variety of perspectives. Short pieces of narrative and 'bubbled' speech captions in child-like language provide an enchanting book.

Nick and Sophie's old cat dies from cat flu. With Mum and Dad's help they bury him in the garden beside the graves of other pets. That night the fantasy begins as the children join in the neighbourhood cats' funeral ceremony, singing 'caterwauling' hymns and learning of Fred's night-time alter ego fame as a music hall turn. Mysteriously, by the next day a gravestone has appeared in the garden, bearing the inscription: *Famous Fred.*

Aspects of bereavement:

- sharing feelings of sadness with others
- facing the fact that death is final
- remembering the happy times together
- showing respect at a funeral
- expressing thanksgiving for the life of deceased
- using gifts or flowers to show sympathy.

Snell, N. (1984) *Emma's Cat Dies*

Another sad yet eventually comforting story of a child's kitten which is run over by a car. Mum grieves with the child and together they remember the good life which they had given to the kitten, how he played, enjoyed his food and loved them. Again, the child chooses to wait a while before having another animal. Simple line and wash illustrations are representational, qualifying each page's message and nothing else.

Aspects of bereavement:

- sharing grief helps
- remembering the good times together.

Wilhelm, H. (1985) *I'll Always Love You*
A small boy's very own dog, Elfie, gradually grows old and fat. The child insists that the dog sleeps in his room. Each night he carries her upstairs, puts her on a soft cushion and whispers, 'I'll always love you.' (opening 11) Emotive water-colour pictures show a grieving family burying the dog in the garden. The child refuses the neighbour's offer of a new puppy but donates Elfie's basket to that puppy. One day he decides he will have another animal and will tell it every night, 'I shall always love you'. (final opening) Softly coloured illustrations echo the text.

Aspects of bereavement:

- children (and adults) feel remorse that they didn't tell the deceased person (or animal) how much they were loved
- children and adults, in the early stages of grieving, find it difficult to cope in places where there have been shared memories with the deceased.

'DEATH' OF A TOY
These two books, Mansell, D. (1993) *My Old Teddy* and Williams, M. (1995) *The Velveteen Rabbit* (originally published 1926) have similar themes, of a much-loved, much-mended toy which over the years gradually falls apart. The teddy has to be thrown away and a new one bought, but the child reminisces over the happy times spent with the old teddy. When the velveteen rabbit has to be thrown away after its owner has scarlet fever the child fantasises that it comes alive again in a new state but cannot belong to him again.

Aspects of bereavement:

- ageing is inevitable
- bodies have to be discarded but the spirit may live on
- fantasising about death.

DEATH OF SIBLING
Dean, A. (1992) *Meggie's Magic*
Delicately coloured illustrations enhance the text of this thirty-page book in which the narrator mourns for her older sister Meggie who died

at the age of eight. The little girl is confused and lonely. Her parents, deep in their own grief, leave her to her own devices. She takes the reader to the places where she and Meggie used to play magic games. She is comforted to find that the magic did not die with Meggie, but remains in spirit. When she tells her parents of her belief, they realise that they have been so wrapped up in their own grief that they had not thought of their child's grief. This story, similar in theme to *Bridge To Terabithia* (Paterson 1977, reviewed on p.74), is directed towards a readership of early teenagers.

Aspects of bereavement:

- searching for comfort
- non-recognition of a small child's grief
- re-creating relationship with deceased.

DEATH OF GRANDPARENT

Anderson, R. (1996) *Letters From Heaven*

This is a charming and unusual story, told with great insight into a child's thoughts. Granny has left a letter to be given to the child after her death. The whole story is told through a pattern of alternating letters, written by the child to her Granny and from Granny in heaven with imaginary addresses such as 'The Great Hereafter', 'Never-never-land' and 'Somewhere Over the Rainbow'. There is a touching portrayal of the child's grief and longing for her Granny. The mother finds the letters and realises how the death has affected the child. '"Oh, my darling, my poor dearest girl." and they both hugged and cried.' (p.69)

Aspects of bereavement:

- the need, sometimes, to continue a relationship in memories
- writing to a deceased person may help children (and adults) to come to terms with the loss
- importance of recognising that children grieve, often secretly
- that a child may need to be given 'permission' to grieve.

Burningham, J. (1984) *Granpa*

Illustrated by the author in soft muted tones, this book is a series of short conversations between a little girl and her Granpa. Together they go fishing, watch TV, sing songs and go on outings. One day Granpa is unwell. The last page, without explanatory text, depicts the little girl and Granpa's empty chair. The reader cannot be certain whether Granpa has died or is away being cared for, making this book suitable for a grieving child or as gentle preparation for the possibility of hospitalisation or death of an elderly person.

Aspect of bereavement:

- whilst there is no overt suggestion of death and grieving this book emphasises the value of shared experiences which can be revived later in memory.

Hathorn, L. (1994) *Grandma's Shoes*

Another instance of a child's fantasy is narrated by a child who, devastated by the death of her grandmother, finds that when she puts on her grandmother's shoes she can re-create their former affinity and relationship. Her imagination enables her to communicate with her grandmother and resolve such problems as the acceptance of the finality of death and coping with grief. This book, illustrated by softly coloured pictures, provides an emotional yet gentle, soothing insight into a child's loss and grief.

Aspects of bereavement:

- memories live on
- fantasising after a death is common among children
- it is acceptable to continue relating to a deceased person.

BASED ON THE CYCLE OF NATURE

The following three books highlight the inevitability and certainty of death but emphasise the positive aspect of the continuity of generations.

Buscaglia, L. (1982) *The Fall of Freddie the Leaf*

Freddie is a brightly coloured leaf on a deciduous tree. He experiences the delights of being 'born' in spring, enjoys the summer of comfort and pleasure, followed by preparation for the autumn in which he and his friends have to change colour, die and leave the tree. But life goes on in the delicate balance of life and death. A book for very young children.

Carle, E. (1974) *The Very Hungry Caterpillar*
This book explains the stages of metamorphosis and eventual death of the butterfly, which has left its eggs behind ready to carry on the next generation. The pictures are clear and beautifully presented in colour.

Stickney, D. (1984) *Waterbugs and Dragonflies*
A story of the various stages in a dragonfly's life, including its inevitable death, this time into a spirit world. The pictures have very clear outlines in black, ready for the child to colour in. A Christian theme runs through the book ending with prayers and an interpretation of the lifecycle.

Fitzgerald, S. (1998) *The Tale of Two Dolphins*
This is actually written by a thirteen-year-old girl five years after the sudden death of her elder sister in a minibus accident. The two girls and their relationship are transposed into dolphins. She tells of their closeness, their escapades and of the time when the elder dolphin suddenly disappeared in the sea. The younger dolphin's appetite waned and she felt locked away from the rest of the world, dreaming of happier times with her sister. One day she met another dolphin with whom she could talk. That led to her being able to talk to her parents. They all cried together, deciding to visit the place where the death occurred. Healing grieving began there. The illustrations are beautifully simple and delicate. The story is suitable for children from six years old but there are also hidden meanings which would make it of comfort to older children.

Aspects of bereavement:
- feeling the need to hide away
- lack of appetite
- not feeling able to talk to parents, often for fear of upsetting them
- ability to talk to someone not in the family.

Recommended for children up to fourteen years

The following books are listed in alphabetical order of author.

Joan Aiken's six collections of short stories, for children of ten to mid-teens, all contain aspects of death, some incidental and some as a major theme. Selections are from *A Goose on your Grave* (1987) and *A Creepy Company* (1993). These stories cover some unusual topics and all contain interesting detail in the plot periphery.

The following three stories may help children who have not openly expressed their own grief but may find relief in grieving openly for a fictitious character.

In *A Goose on your Grave* the story of *Wing Quack Flap* (**Mild**) set in the North of England, tells of Pat, who is orphaned by the death of his parent and has to leave Ireland to live with his crotchety grandfather and eccentric aunt. When 'Granda' refuses to let the boy have a pet for company, his aunt invites him to share her imaginary pet duck (the title name) which 'lives' in a Chinese teapot. In the feverishness of a 'flu attack Pat hallucinates for days, pouring out all his grief to the duck. As Granda is led away after assaulting the police, a loud quacking is heard, fading into the distance. Pat has resolved his grief.

Aspect of bereavement:

- telling one's feelings to an imaginary friend or an inanimate object can bring relief in grief.

The Snow Horse (**Mod**) tells of Cal, a lame foundling, rescued from a snowdrift which had buried his parents. As Cal loves horses he is given the care of a sick horse left by a traveller. His instructions are to bury it under a rowan tree if it dies, but first to pluck three hairs from its mane and keep them. Cal is distraught when his cruel boss buries the horse in the muck heap so he secretly re-buries its bones and makes a snow-horse in its memory. As he ties a hair round the snow-horse's neck the magic begins. One set of footprints lead to the door but not away again. Cal disappears; the snow-horse too. A heart-tugging story for children who love horses.

Aspect of bereavement:

- adhering to a ritual can appear essential to relieve feelings and leave the past behind.

Lob's Girl (**Mod**) also in *A Goose on your Grave*, is another heart-tugging story, which will appeal to dog-loving children. Aiken shows her talent for detail, describing the dog, Lob, as topaz-eyed with black-tipped pricked ears, a thick soft coat and a bushy black-tipped tail. He and Sandy, aged fourteen, are devoted to each other. When out walking together, Sandy is knocked down by a lorry and gravely injured. In hospital she murmurs 'Lob', puts her hand out of bed, strokes his wet ears, turns over and goes to sleep. But Lob had been killed at the time of the accident!

Aspect of bereavement:

- creating comfort by imagining the deceased is present.

Aiken's story, *Die From Day to Day* (**Mod**) in *A Creepy Company* describes a situation with which many children could identify, that of a family travelling on the motorway returning from a holiday. The mother is becoming exasperated with the three girls bickering on the back seat. Then the girls begin to discuss two deaths in which their father was involved. He had knocked over and killed a drunken man and had also been responsible, as a planning officer, for the death of an old woman who had been bricked up in her condemned house. The father begins to reminisce in his own mind, thinking back to his granny's tales about an old washerwoman who, if she catches your eye, casts a spell. Suddenly the car stops. '"This is where I quit!" says the father' (p.142). He leaves the car, runs down an embankment and sees an old washerwoman who turns and tells him, '"You will die from day to day"' (p.146). Aiken leaves the ending open for interpretation by the reader.

Aspects of bereavement:

- children's failure to close an incident of death
- persistent guilt leading to breakdown.

In *The End of Silence* (**Mod**) (in *A Creepy Company*) Aiken demonstrates her deep insight into possible experiences of teenagers following a death of a parent. Ned, the main protagonist, narrates the story of how the death of his mother, killed in a bomb incident at Frankfurt airport, has affected his family. He becomes addicted to eating tortilla crisps, 'bag after bag', and reading murder mysteries from second-hand paper-backs, 'book after book'. His sister remains silent. His father shuts himself away from the others, talking endlessly to his pet owl. When Ned's and his sister's plan to kill the owl misfires and it is killed instead by an excavator, they suffer deep guilt as their father falls deeper into his grief. The owl continues to haunt the children.

Aspects of bereavement:

- differing responses to a sudden death
- hate for something or someone who alienates a formerly loving relationship
- guilt and subsequent imagined haunting.

Aiken's use of spiritual references appears again in *The Whispering Mountain* (1968) (**Mod**). As an old man is dying the reader hears that, 'Suddenly his eyes brightened, and for a moment, opened wide as if he saw something very beautiful and unexpected directly in front of him. "Oh, well now, fancy that!" he exclaimed and was gone' (p.214).

Aspect of death and bereavement:

- the moment of death is commonly reported by attending relatives and if children are present it may be used to give comfort.

Hollindale (1974) in *Choosing Books For Children* praises Aiken for her boldness in portraying death so practically in this book.

In Aiken's short story *The Green Arches* (in *Mooncake*) (**Mod**) the narrator, a handicapped teenage boy, is able to transcend towards a spiritual world through green arches of trees, found when he had been through a near-death experience. His brother, Bran, after a serious accident is in intensive care and not expected to live. The transcendental ritual leads the handicapped boy through the green arches into a place filled with peace and light where he joins Bran.

Aspect of bereavement:

- A story with deep spiritual connotations.

In *Your Mind is a Mirror* (**Mild**) (in *A Goose on Your Grave*, Aiken), Sam feels hatred for his deeply depressed and recently widowed father who hardly notices Sam's presence. Sam needs comforting, needs to talk about his mother and to express his feelings but there is no one to listen. He shouts, "'I hate him, why doesn't he jump in and drown'" (p.30). Eventually the two share their grief.

Aspects of bereavement:

- emotional loneliness
- the need to talk about a deceased parent
- outbursts of shouting are quite common in grief – may prove cathartic
- hate for remaining parent.

Atkinson, E. (1940) *Greyfriars Bobby* (**Mod**)
This appealing story tells of a dog in mourning for its dead master. This story, although not written within the time period of the majority of the chosen books in this study, has been re-issued by four publishers in the 1990s. The writer employs dialogue in the Scottish vernacular which may make for a difficult read for this age group, although there are inter-pretative footnotes provided.

Aspect of bereavement:

- highlighting of the close emotional relationship between dog and owner.

As grief is centred on the dog's responses this book could be used as a trigger story, i.e. to release a child's unresolved grief in a non-human context.

Bawden, N. (1985) *The Finding* (**Mild**)
This story tells of suspended grieving. An adopted child of eleven is left
a large sum of money by an old woman who believes the boy to be the
child of her missing daughter. When he finally lays the ghost of his
mother to rest he goes to sit in the arms of the Sphinx on the Embankment where he had been found as a baby.

In another of Bawden's books, *The Real Plato Jones* (1994) (**Emo**), the
young teenager Plato accompanies his mother to Greece to attend his
grandfather's funeral, and is shocked when confronted with Greek
customs. He is very apprehensive and is horrified that he will be
expected to kiss the corpse goodbye. He also fears that he will show his
embarrassment at the behaviour of his relatives who may well throw
themselves into the grave, screaming and sobbing. At the funeral Plato
is ashamed when he feels faint, is loaded on to a donkey cart and taken
away. The reader is allowed close access to Plato's fear and trepidation.
This is a book strong in emotions and coping tactics.

Aspects of bereavement:

- fear of touching a dead person
- apprehension at attending a funeral
- embarrassment at others' behaviour.

Baur, M.D. (1987) *On My Honour* (**Mod**)
A daredevil prank in a treacherous river ends in a drowning. One boy
invents a story to cover up the truth but when the body is not found he is
consumed with guilt. A story told with understanding and empathy.

Aspect of bereavement:

- feelings of blame and guilt.

Bunting, E. (2000) *Blackwater* (**Mod**)
Set in California by a raging river, the story is told by Brodie, a
thirteen-year-old boy racked by guilt, having caused the death by
drowning of two of his peers, a girl and a boy, although he did try to
save them. Alex, the boy's cousin, lies about the cause of the accident,

making out that Brodie is a hero, which drives him into deeper guilt feelings. An anonymous letter arrives with one word on the page – TELL. Brodie has hallucinations and dreams that the dead boy comes back to haunt him. Another minor but touching reference to bereavement comes from a girl who befriends Brodie, who tells him of her feelings when her mother died. It is this girl who has sent the letter because of her worry over a tragedy and it led to confession and eventual peace.

Aspects of bereavement:

- intense guilt leading to disruption of normal life
- hallucinations
- nightmares
- confession may bring peace
- loving support from parents after confession.

Byars, B. (1980) *The Night Swimmers* (**Mild**)
Retta, aged twelve, acting as mother to her two younger brothers since their real mother died in a plane crash two years previously, speaks of the unswallowed, unspoken pain of her mother's death. The pain seemed to stay in her throat for such a long time that she thought she would die of it. Her brother, aged seven when his mother died, had mourned for a long time, sitting crying for hours in the wardrobe amongst his mother's clothes. Their father leaves the children to their own devices and they sneak off every night to swim in a private pool. When the younger boy nearly drowns the owner rescues him and confronts the father with his responsibility. The writer gives a good insight into children's grief although the story line is rather weak. There is little conflict or tension to arouse a reader's attention, and closure – when the father decides to marry with the full approval of the children – seems ineffectual.

Aspects of bereavement:

- responsibility of a child assuming a deceased parent's role

- difficulty of young children accepting an older child's authority

- variation in mode of grieving in different children.

Byars, B. (1979) *Goodbye, Chicken Little* (**Mod**)

Jimmie Little's father is killed in a coalmine accident. On the night before his death Jimmie has a violent argument with him, an incident which has left him with a heavy feeling of guilt. Without his father he feels 'like a snail turned out of his shell' (p.26) and opts out of many activities, hence his self-appointed name, 'Chicken'. He sees his eccentric, drunken Uncle Pete fall through the ice on a frozen river while attempting to cross it for a dare. This scene is vividly described with gripping moments of emotion. His mother at first blames Jimmie for not stopping him. Again, guilt grips him, causing him to sink into apathy. It is not until he goes to a party to celebrate Uncle Pete's life that Jimmie finally learns to appreciate the good times and put the bad times behind him. This is a story that would probably appeal to ten- to twelve-year-old boys.

Aspects of bereavement:

- guilt over death having occurred without reconciliation after an argument

- having unearned blame thrust upon one in anger

- importance of remembering the good times.

Fuller, J. (1993) *John's Book* (**Emo**)

This book is written with a deep compassionate understanding of a bereaved child's feelings. John, aged twelve, dreads having to attend his father's funeral, not knowing how to behave or what might happen. When he panics at the sudden thought that his mother might die too he makes excuses to stay away from school. The story spans about a year during which John suffers behavioural aberrations typical of bereaved children. The question of a bereaved parent meeting a new potential partner is raised when John's mother brings home a widower and his small daughter to spend their first Christmas since bereavement together. John throws tantrums and storms off, threatening to leave home. The writer's account of the moment of realisation in releasing the past and facing a new future is moving, understandable and could be comforting to any bereaved child. The two children spend their Christmas together, sharing an unspoken empathy. John's aunt gives him a book of their family history. As he puts in photos of his mother, her new husband, himself and step-sister, he writes MY NEW FAMILY.

Aspects of bereavement:

- disbelief after a sudden death
- need for 'permission' to cry
- school refusal through fear of second death
- behaviour quite out of character
- anger, bewilderment, relationship problems
- facing rehabilitation within a new normal life
- fear of a new partner taking the place of a deceased parent.

Hamilton, V. (1990) *Cousins* (**Emo**)

This intense story recounts the jealousy of two cousins, particularly over best friends. One cousin is drowned while saving a friend. The other cousin, feeling somewhat responsible, grieves deeply, retreating from her normal life, refusing to speak or eat. Only after many months, with the help of her family, does she gradually begin to recover.

Aspects of bereavement:

- effects of guilt disrupting normal life
- accepting help from others to overcome grief symptoms.

Hoy, L. (1981) *Your Friend Rebecca* (**Emo**)

This is written from a particularly personal focus as Rebecca, aged twelve or thirteen, narrates her own story, set in a school and home situation. She tells of her turmoil since her mother died. Her father in his grief has no time for her and turns to drink. Rebecca admits her bad behaviour, her frustrations and her rudeness. She describes her numbness, her feelings of rejection, hopelessness and depression. The author brings a real-life believable aspect into the story with the printing of 'hand-written' letters between Rebecca and her father whilst she is on a school trip to France. This story of humour and pathos has a satisfactory outcome when Rebecca and her father realise that if they share their pain, misery and anguish they will also share hope. The writer, being a teacher herself, shows deep understanding of a child's mind, using language and syntax at 'child' level.

Aspects of bereavement:

- emotional loneliness
- rejection by remaining parent
- hate for remaining parent
- behavioural problems.

Little, J. (1984) *Mama's Going to Buy You a Mockingbird* (**Emo**)
A third-person narrator takes the reader through one family's response to terminal illness and death. As an observer the reader is free to opt in and out of the story as may be identifiable or emotionally bearable within his or her own experience. Jeremy, aged twelve, and his younger sister are sent away while their father undergoes surgery. They have picked up signs that all is not well and show typical pre-teen signs of anxiety. Mum tells Jeremy of his father's impending death and, 'Then without another word, he was in his mother's arms, hugged up close against her and they were crying together' (p.88).

Aspects of grief and bereavement:

- it's all right for boys to show their emotion
- picking up signals that all is not well
- talking to a pet for comfort
- uncertainty in how to answer people's questions
- value of talking to others of similar experience
- the value of having a mutually loved keepsake for remembrance.

Mayfield, S. (1990) *I Carried You on Eagles' Wings* (**Emo**)
This book is recommended by Cruse Bereavement Care for seven- to thirteen-year-olds but it is quite suitable for older teenagers.

Tony, aged twelve, the only child of a vicar, has always had to help his mother who is slowly dying from the effects of multiple sclerosis. He builds up intense hate, for himself, his father, his mother, his grand-mother and for the people who ask how his mother is when they know she is dying. Very emotional scenes are described in such graphic detail that children bereaved in a similar way can closely identify with Tony. Although the main theme of this story is based on the mother's illness and death, it is well balanced by reference to Tony's school activities, his care for an injured seagull and his awakening romantic feelings for a girl who befriends him.

Aspects of bereavement:

- regret at not letting deceased person know of love for her
- sharing emotion
- acceptance that men and boys do cry
- children should not be excluded from important discussions
- wish for adults to answer questions honestly.

Newman, M. (1995) *Steve* (**Emo**)
When Steve, in his final year of junior school, is called to the headmas-ter's office he learns that his father has had an accident at work. Mother drives the five children to the hospital only to learn that Dad has died. His sister Gemma reacts with shouting and screaming but Steve remains silent in shock. Later on Steve wants to see where the accident had happened and although he wants to know where Dad's body is and what it looks like he dare not ask. Each member of the family writes a letter to place in the coffin. Steve hates the funeral, tries not to notice Mum's tears. Steve does badly at school, argues with his siblings and tries to assume part of Dad's role to keep his presence alive. Gemma is also in trouble at school, refusing to listen to adults and adopting an attitude of indifference in lessons. Once again, in a story reflecting true

life, this boy works through his grief, growing emotionally as he cares for a kitten which he has rescued. Bereaved children would recognise the behavioural problems typical in the aftermath of a bereavement. The writer weaves a great deal of factual material into a believable story, including aspects of death and bereavement that adults commonly fail to address.

Aspects of bereavement:

- varying reactions to sudden death
- curiosity about a dead body
- wanting to view place of death
- dread of attending funeral
- aberrant behaviour
- being needed by an animal or person helps to overcome sorrow.

Paterson, K. (1977) *Bridge To Terabithia* (**Mod**)
Set in a rural community near Washington, USA, this fast moving story pivots on the central character, Jess, aged about ten. The third-person omniscient narrator addresses many issues of concern to pre-adolescents, describing Jess's thoughts as he passes through events and feelings typical of his age group. He feels unloved, has outbursts of hate, bullies his peers, hero-worships others and has crushes on his teachers. A friendship develops with a girl, Leslie. Together they create a fantasy land (Terabithia) in a secret place reached by swinging on a rope across a ravine. One day Leslie, going alone, slips into the torrent and drowns. When Jess suffers deep grief and fails to express his grief openly he returns to Terabithia, rekindles his fantasy and gradually comes to terms with his loss. Jess is forced to confront his own purpose in life and his character grows in personality and maturity as he finds his true identity.

Aspects of bereavement:

- the expectation that boys will not grieve
- upset caused by bereavement at time of puberty problems
- reliving previous events which give comfort.

Rowling, J.K. (1997) *Harry Potter and the Philosopher's Stone* (**Mild**)
Baby Harry Potter is left on his aunt's doorstep after his parents, a witch and wizard, are killed by an evil member. of their community. Harry suffers a 'Cinderella' upbringing until he goes to a school of witchcraft. There, in a magic mirror, he sees a group of green-eyed people standing behind him – he is looking at his family for the first time! His mother is waving, smiling, yet also crying. Harry turns around but there is no one there. At the time he has a powerful ache inside him, half joy and half terrible sadness. Afterwards he has nightmares in which his parents disappear in a flash of green light accompanied by a high-pitched cackle. At the end of the school year Harry is presented with a handsome leather book. In it is a collection of photographs of his parents. When asked if he liked the book we are told, 'Harry couldn't speak but Hagrid understood' (p.220).

Aspects of bereavement:

- sense of not belonging
- confronting pictures or stories of unknown parents
- nightmares after knowing tragic cause of death of parents
- mixed emotions when realising what has been missed.

Smith, D.B. (1975) *A Taste of Blackberries* (**Emo**)
A first-person narrator, whose name we never know, although we get to know a lot about him, tells of the tragic death of Jamie, his best friend whom he watched die from anaphylactic shock following a bee sting. The boy has to face the tragedy, the funeral and the guilt that perhaps he might have saved Jamie if he had known about his allergy. He cannot imagine the immediate future without his friend. Written as such a personal story the reader can enter the mind of this boy, learning of his innermost thoughts and actions told in a childlike way. The time span covers only a few weeks.

Aspects of bereavement:

- denial of event of death
- 'conversation' with dead person

- feelings of guilt

- anger and frustration with self and adults

- secret outbursts of crying

- fear of provoking crying in others, particularly adults

- desire to receive and give comfort

- apathy and loss of appetite

- final acceptance of death.

White, E.B. (1963) *Charlotte's Web* (**Mild**)
This book tells of a little girl's love for a runt piglet (Wilbur) and the piglet's friendship with a spider (Charlotte) and a rat. Charlotte's death scene is quite sad, causing Wilbur to throw himself to the ground, 'in an agony of pain and sorrow', and 'great sobs racked his body' (p.155). The spider accepts the advance of death as an inevitable natural part of life's pattern. Wilbur ensures the succession of spiders by carrying the egg sac containing five hundred and fourteen babies back to the barn where Charlotte came from. White's vivid descriptions of seasonal changes provide detailed information that could capture and extend a child's interest in the countryside. Child readers commented on several of his descriptions, including one of a foggy morning when he likens the grass to a magic carpet and the asparagus patch to a silver forest, and also on Charlotte's web which, '...glistened in the light and made a pattern of loveliness and mystery like a delicate veil' (p.73).

Aspects of bereavement:

- life always ends in death

- it's all right to grieve openly

- it helps to carry the deceased person in one's memory.

The death of a creature as portrayed in *Charlotte's Web* and *Greyfriars Bobby* may be emotionally charged, but it is not as sensitive an issue as an account of a human death.

Froggy's Little Brother by 'Brenda' (see p.30) (**Emo**) and its parallel contemporary story *Two Weeks With the Queen* by Gleitzman (**Mod**) (Fig: 3.1 p.39) described in Chapter 2 (p.38) are also suitable for this age group, as is *Squib* by Nina Bawden (**Mild**) (reviewed in detail in Chapter 6).

Recommended for older teenagers

Blume, J. (1981) *Tiger Eyes* (**Mod**)
Typical teenage behaviour patterns are well presented in this fast moving story which opens as a girl of fifteen witnesses the shooting of her father. She can't cope, can't deal with the finality of his death until she breaks away from her normal life and goes to stay with her aunt. In disobedience typical of a grieving teenager, she builds up a relationship of mutual support with an emotionally disturbed young man. As she finds relief in baring her innermost thoughts she begins to fall in love. Dialogue, which plays a prominent part in the story, is lively, realistic and uses language suited to the protagonists' age group. The story is left open-ended.

Aspects of bereavement:

- reliving the horror of witnessing a violent death
- lack of support from family
- evading facing up to reality
- need for releasing tension by 'talking it out', often with a stranger.

Branfield, J. (1981) *Fox in Winter* (**Mild**)
A fifteen-year-old fatherless girl befriends an elderly couple visited by her district nurse mother. The girl tries to share their feelings when they refuse to move to an old people's home, but their stubbornness eventually causes their deaths in miserable loneliness. The girl struggles with her conscience and feelings to rationalise the outcome and to find her own identity.

Aspect of bereavement:

- guilt, self-blame for a death and an inability to alter course of events.

Dalton, A. (1992) *Naming the Dark* (**Mod**)

The reader is given comprehensive biographies of the main teenage characters, together with an excellent perspective of personal relationships. Some readers will empathise with the protagonist's situation, particularly his parents' divorce and his friend's death. Several readers commented on the slow start which, in a book of two hundred and thirty pages, does not draw the reader into the story quickly enough to incite motivation to reach the end. However, there is an exciting climax when the main character finally realises that he is not the loser he once thought he was.

Aspects of bereavement:

- talking to deceased person
- hallucinations of bringing the deceased person back
- feeling of abandonment.

Grant, C. (1996) *Shadow Man* (**Emo**)

An eighteen-year-old boy dies in a car accident, casting a shadow over the lives of many people who knew him. The story tends to be fragmented by the writer's unusual choice of eleven personal narrators who recount their own feelings, all focused on the dead boy. Tensions are high, emotions are deep, all well documented in the mode of each character. When read several times the chapters gel into a hauntingly believable story.

Aspect of bereavement:

- death viewed from adults' and teenagers' angles.

Hill, D. (1992) *See Ya, Simon* (**Emo**)

Written by a New Zealand high school teacher and based in a school setting, this story offers a deeply sensitive insight into the interpersonal relationships of children, parents and teachers when faced with an anticipated death. The storyline is strong and fast moving. Nathan, Simon's best friend, narrates the story of this young teenager's last year of life, telling of Simon's courage and emotional strength as his physical strength ebbs due to muscular dystrophy. However, this is not a morbid story, as Simon's wicked sense of humour and his supreme effort to live life to the end prove uplifting. Aged fourteen, Simon dies. His friends view him in his coffin and the whole of his class attends the funeral. Didacticism is both direct, in the narrator's description of muscular dystrophy, and indirect, told through dialogue and Simon's behaviour.

Aspects of bereavement:

- dying youngster's attitude towards anticipated death
- attitudes of peers towards anticipated death
- attitudes of adults towards dying person and towards his peers
- viewing the body and attending the funeral.

Johnson, P. (1989) *We, the Haunted* (**Mod**)

The two main characters narrate the story in alternating chunks, carrying the reader in the present tense, which gives the story a strong sense of urgency. Dialogue at the beginning of the book provides a lively banter before the death by drowning of the girl's beloved boyfriend, but after that event the narration and dialogue become more solemn and deep. This highlights the way life changes after bereavement, particularly the common feelings or hallucinations that the deceased is still around.

Aspects of bereavement:

- apparent change of character after bereavement
- hallucinations perpetuated by bereaved person
- withdrawal from normal life

- eventual acceptance of death and creation of a new mode of life.

Lloyd, C. (1989) *The Charlie Barber Treatment* (**Emo**)

Fifteen-year-old Simon finds his mother dead on his return from school. Like many bereaved youngsters, particularly boys, he suppresses his grief, clams up, rejects his friends and refuses to go out with them, but gives the outward appearance of coping well. By chance Simon meets sixteen-year-old Charlie [Charlotte] Barber, a bright, bubbly girl who is not put off by Simon's uncouth, negative attitude. A teenage romance begins, but when Charlie has to return to her home many miles away Simon again feels desolate and grief-stricken. At this point he breaks down and in Charlie's arms he sobs out all his former grief. This is an open-ended story and the reader is left to speculate on the continued friendship of Simon and Charlie.

Aspects of bereavement:

- hiding true feelings
- effects of failing to grieve, particularly on boys
- advantages of openly declaring feelings within a 'safe' situation.

Mahy, M. (1995) *Memory* (**Emo**)

This is a story of deep human emotions, of guilt and mental turmoil. Jonny is haunted by the death of his sister, but fails to come to terms with his grief. Leaving home after an argument he encounters Sophie, wandering in the confusion of Alzheimer's Disease. She has no memory; he has too strong a memory. She mistakes him for a nephew and he takes refuge with her. Their time together changes both their lives in a way neither of them had foreseen. In becoming responsible for Sophie, Jonny finds his own identity. Mahy shows sensitivity and understanding of teenagers in her description of Jonny's misery.

Aspects of bereavement:

- lasting feelings of unwarranted guilt over a death

- unwillingness to talk about problems

- inability to cope with normal life

- escape from the situation is not the way to re-establish normal life

- being needed can bring about rehabilitation.

Matthews, A. (1995) *Seeing in Moonlight* (**Emo**)
Three sixth-formers who enjoyed a strong friendship tell of the impact which the death of one of them, killed by a hit-and-run driver, has had on their lives. This is a fast moving, witty and emotional story written with a deep understanding of older teenagers. The dialogue is expressively vernacular, lending a true-to-life atmosphere to events.

Aspects of bereavement:

- coping with sudden death

- effects of losing one of a small close-knit group

- finding comfort in sharing grief with others

- building a memory bank of the deceased person.

Strachan, I. (1993) *The Boy in the Bubble* (**Emo**)
A male author 'becomes' a female narrator, skilfully relating the growing love affair between a teenage girl and a boy who, because of his illness, has to live within the controlled atmosphere of a plastic tent. This central theme is well supported with scenes within both school and home situations. The conclusion is particularly poignant when the boy comes out of his 'bubble', the two teenagers become lovers and the boy dies.

Aspects of bereavement:

- coping with anticipated death – early grieving

- cherishing memories.

Talbert, M. (1988) *Dead Birds Singing* (**Emo**) A book with powerfully deep emotions. A fatherless teenager suffers a double tragedy when his mother is killed instantly in a car crash and his older sister dies later. The boy moves to his best friend's home but finds it difficult to adjust to a happy family situation.

Aspects of bereavement:

- effects of losing 'anchor' person in one's life
- feeling of wanting to die to join deceased person
- difficulty in accepting offers of help
- feeling that no one else knows how one feels.

Wilson, J. (1989) *Falling Apart* (**Emo**)
A third-person narrator invites the reader as a close observer to share this story of desperation, passion, sensitivity and empathy. The plot outlines teenage Tina's reaction to the death of her twin brother many years previously and her first love affair which breaks up, causing deep despair and attempted suicide. The story opens as the girl makes careful preparations to take an overdose: the description is elaborate, drawn out and harrowing. The final chapter is set in the hospital as Tina recovers. In between is the account of the events leading up to her decision to end her life. Home conditions are traumatic; Tina's parents ban any reference to her deceased brother Tim, her mother swallows Valium tablets 'like Smarties', her elder sister is married and lives away and her other sister is immersed in her A-level exams. All this leaves Tina unhappily struggling to find her true identity. She suffers terrifying nightmares, which are described in horrific detail. Tina is flattered by the attentions of a boy from a local select private school. Although she cherishes her first sexual experience in the cemetery, guilt returns as she imagines her brother watching. Unfortunately the boy grows tired of Tina's demanding ways and drops her, precipitating her 'falling apart' and attempted suicide. The story is vividly told, rich in detail and expands the basic plot into an intimate study of family life, class differences, relationships and interactions.

Aspects of bereavement:

- inability to resolve persistent guilt over death of sibling
- jealousy of sibling, post-death
- effects of being misunderstood by family
- inability to talk about problems.

Worral, A. (1985) *A Flash of Blue* (**Emo**)
A teenage girl and her little brother have been told that their father has only a few months to live until cancer ends his life. There is intense sadness at first, followed by the decision to make family life as normal and happy as possible. This book is written with great sensitivity and insight into each family member's response to the realisation of the shortening time available for being together. Their discussions reinforce their decision to live life to its fullest potential and will provide comforting reassurance to the reader.

Aspects of bereavement:

- family decisions
- accepting pre-death grief
- memories to be cherished
- resolve to make remaining time as rich as possible.

Fictionalised fact books

There cannot be any 'facts' about children's reactions to bereavement, only what is observed by adults and related by the children. Each person has a unique response to bereavement.

Most of the following books were written purposely to help children cope with bereavement, explaining about death and possible expected reactions, presented within a believable sequential story.

For young children

Green, W. (1989) *Gran's Grave*

Each page has a softly tinted illustration which enhances the emotional atmosphere of this story which begins with the death and 'funeral' of a pet gerbil. When Grandad visits he feels for the loneliness of the gerbil's mate and remarks on his hope to see Gran when he gets to heaven. The child questions the existence of an after-life. As Grandad tends Gran's grave, helped by his grandson, he reminisces over his relationship with her. When the child reads the inscription on her tombstone expressing love he decides to write a similar one on a lollipop stick for his gerbil. The story is intimately presented mainly through dialogue.

Nystrom, C. (1990) *Emma Says Goodbye*

Simple illustrations provide a powerful supplement to this book, qualifying and enhancing the text. Emma's aunt comes to stay to recuperate after her chemotherapy. Emma is shocked by her appearance, so thin and without hair, but realises that Auntie Sue still retains a zest for life. Together they have fun and adventures by the river and begin a patchwork quilt, working on it every day while they chat. Eventually Auntie Sue is confined to bed, unable to eat, too weak to move and needing oxygen inhalation. Illustrations show the family gathered in prayer around the bed when she dies. Although Emma says goodbye at the funeral she feels close to Auntie Sue as she works to complete the quilt.

Padoan, G. (1987) *Remembering Grandad*

This is written with a refreshing approach emphasising the positive aspects of cohesive family mourning. The children are included in arrangements for the funeral, asked to choose flowers and write letters to Grandad remembering the happy time they spent together. Illustrations, several from an 'angel's' viewpoint, (or is it Grandad's?) depict the progression of the funeral from the semi-detached house to the crematorium.

Wadell, M. (1990) *Grandma's Bill*
Simple uncluttered illustrations support this short text, which tells of a child visiting her grandmother and enquiring about a photograph. She cannot grasp the concepts of ageing, dying at a young age or different generations. The child, snuggled in the comfort of her grandmother's arms, learns from very clear explanations based on an album of photographs.

Lamont, S. (1989) *Ewen's Little Brother*
Ewen, who from the simple, colourful crayon-type pictures looks about three-and-a-half to four years old, has a baby brother, Gavin. When Gavin becomes terminally ill (presumably with cancer as the publication is supported by the Newcastle Children's Cancer Unit) and is taken to hospital, Ewen sees the hospital staff making every effort to cure him. But, as the book relates in straightforward language for a small child to understand, 'They tried very hard to make him better but one day Gavin died. It was no one's fault, he was just too ill to live. The next page tells that 'They knew he was in heaven…and did not need his body any more so it was buried' (opening 8). Opposite is a picture of the funeral procession entering the church. The final picture shows Ewen looking at photographs of Gavin and smiling as the text informs us, 'He is very glad to have had a little brother' (last page). It is often difficult for a parent to prepare a small child for a younger child's death in the family and this would be a valuable book to be read in such a situation. The message is direct and factual but in a gentle down-to-earth presentation.

Aspects of bereavement:

- sometimes children die from illness – no one is to blame
- death brings relief and release from illness
- it is all right to feel sad at times
- even if you wish to be with the dead person you cannot
- remember the happy times together.

Perkins, G. and Morris, L. (1991) *Remembering Mum*
This book of twenty pages tells the true story of a father and his two small sons, Sam aged five and Eddy aged six. Mum had died the previous year. The narrative is simple and descriptive and is supported by real photograph pictures. The text 'Sometimes Sam feels really sad when he thinks about his mum. But today he feels happy, just remembering how beautiful she was...' (p.6) is illustrated by a photograph showing father and sons looking at a photograph album. Each page depicts an aspect of grieving applicable to small children with an assurance that it is all right to feel like that. The teacher lets the children plant their mother's favourite flowers in the school garden where the boys used to sit quietly and think about their mother. A photograph shows the scene.

The mother, Mandy, is buried in a cemetery near home. A picture shows the father cuddling his sons at the graveside. The supporting text is: '"I know it hurts, boys,"' Dad says, '"but we have each other and we'll always have Mandy in our hearts"' (p.16) and 'Dad usually has a little cry at Mandy's grave' (p17).

Aspects of bereavement:

- it's all right to feel sad
- share sadness with someone
- it's all right to cry openly
- find a special place to remember someone
- reassurance of continuity of lifestyle.

Hollins, S. and Sireling, L. (1989) *When Dad Died* and *When Mum Died*
The authors are both consultant psychiatrists with a particular interest in bereaved children. These 'twin' books are illustrated in bold outlines and bright colours by Elizabeth Webb, a psychology graduate specialising in colour and mime. Produced in conjunction with St George's Hospital, London, the purpose of the books is, according to the writers, to enable children to learn about death before coming face to face with such a trauma. The twenty-eight pages of each book are almost identical – except that there is a man and cremation in one book and a woman

and burial in the other. Facts are presented simply and clearly. The description of death is basic and direct: stopping breathing, being unable to eat, move, walk, speak or see anyone, the body being of no use any more and therefore disposed of.

Aspects of bereavement:

- it's all right to be angry
- losing one's appetite is normal
- acceptance that the deceased's body is of no use
- everyone is sad but not everyone shows grief
- permission to cry – adults cry too.

For older children

Bryant-Mole, K. (1992) *Death*

This is one of a series of seven multicultural informative books with an overall title 'What's Happening'. Each of the twelve chapters, well supported by emotive photographic pictures, takes a separate bereavement issue and answers many of the questions that children ask when they are bereaved or hear of a death. The chapters cover a variety of situations:

1. Loss of dog – the family cried and cried when they remembered the puppy stage.

2. Great-great grandmother dies – explanation of the body wearing out in extreme old age.

3. Mum dies – mentions a child's common fear that the other parent will die too. Suggestion that arrangements be made for child to phone from school each lunchtime for reassurance that other parent is safe.

4. Child's guilt over grandfather's death – in a temper tantrum the week prior to his death a child had wished him dead and blamed himself for the tragedy.

5. Asian child who felt angry with everyone after her mother died. Reassurance that it was all right to be angry – advice on

relieving tension – shouting, beating a pillow, kicking a football.

6. Boy denies that death has taken place. General explanation of burial and cremation being a way of saying goodbye and accepting the finality of death.

7. An eleven-year-old girl worries how they will manage without Dad's income – will they have to leave their home – will she have to leave her friends and school?

8. 'Sees' her brother bleeding to death – everyone is too upset to talk to her.

9. Greg, aged 12, is afraid to mention his dead Mum for fear of upsetting Dad. He also sometimes talked to Mum as if she was still there. Dad said he did too – child given 'permission' to do that.

10. Dean's sister, Katie, dies after a long illness – child feels he isn't ready to accept her predicted death when she dies. Dad suggests drawing his thoughts out on paper. (Art therapy)

11. Helen's baby brother had died a year ago due to a heart defect. The family lit a candle for his birthday and everyone cried.

12. The final chapter suggests keeping some of the deceased's clothes and belongings to remind them of the joy and happiness in the time they had spent together.

Aspects of bereavement:

- permission to cry
- sharing grief
- don't block out that person's life
- celebrate anniversaries with positive thoughts
- find someone to talk to about the dead person
- it's all right to be angry – relieve that anger
- it's all right to 'talk' to the dead person

- express thoughts of insecurity
- pets are like people so you cry when they die
- what you say doesn't cause a death
- seek reassurance when one feels guilty.

Amos, J. (1990) *Sad*

This book is part of a series dealing with negative emotions. (Others are *Afraid*, *Angry*, *Hurt*, *Jealous* and *Lonely*.) There is a third-person narrator but from time to time the author breaks through, addressing the reader directly, asking questions or making comments, such as, 'What would you do now if you were Ella?' (p 25) or, '…you may keep hoping that the dead person will come back, although you know they can't' (p. 30).

Aspects of bereavement:

- being left out of funeral arrangements
- resentment at relative coming to live with family
- declaring feelings
- facing denial of death.

Haughton, E. (1995) *Dealing With Death*

This is a particularly comprehensive book dealing with many aspects of bereavement that appear in the fiction discussed in Chapter 5.

The author acts as an informer, taking real situation examples of bereaved teenagers, in most instances with photographs of the actual youngsters.

1. Alice is sixteen; her brother was killed in a motorcycle accident. She hated the funeral, didn't know how to act, kept thinking that she should cry like everyone else but felt too full to cry so didn't.

2. Peter's mother dies of cancer when he is fourteen. He cannot believe it until he sees her in her coffin. He is hesitant to do so but when he plucks up courage to do so he knows that it isn't really his mother lying there, only her body. (This situation is

also portrayed in *Mama's Going to Buy You a Mockingbird* (Little 1984) and *I Carried You on Eagles' Wings* (Mayfield 1990).)

3. Julian, aged thirteen, also suffers in his grief when his mother dies. He covers up his emotions and appears to get on with life. However, his repressed grief manifests itself in rudeness, bad behaviour and fighting in school. He begins to develop physical symptoms: a hollow feeling, lump in his throat, weakness and susceptibility to infection and breathlessness. (These reactions also appear in the novels *Goodbye, Chicken Little* (Byars 1979) and *The Charlie Barber Treatment* (Lloyd 1989.)

4. Anna's mother dies of cancer after two years of illness. Her father is too preoccupied with his own grieving, and expects Anna, aged fourteen, to take over the mother's role in cooking, cleaning and looking after her little brother and sister. Her schoolwork suffers because she 'mitches' school in order to have some time to herself. (Again, this aspect is taken up in *Your Friend Rebecca* (Hoy 1981).)

5. Tim, aged twelve, had always felt inferior to his older brother who was clever and popular. When the brother is killed in a road accident Tim feels relief at not having to live in his brother's shadow any more. Guilt gradually overtakes his life until he confesses to his friend and releases his feelings. (This aspect appears in *Squib* (Bawden 1980) and *Goodbye, Chicken Little* (Byars 1979).)

Other accounts deal with the death of pets, the care of bereaved friends and the guilt of teenagers at using drugs and alcohol.

Aspects of bereavement:

*   grieving people often become physically ill and/or depressed
*   bereaved parent wishing to marry again
*   role change unsuitable to age of child
*   release of anger
*   loss of temper.

CHAPTER 6

A detailed study
of the novel 'Squib'

Squib, described by Tucker (1981) as 'the most harrowing of Nina Bawden's books for children...' (p.148), is in my opinion outstanding as a book choice for any child within the ages of nine and fourteen years who is trying to come to terms with a bereavement but is not showing any severe grief reactions, signs of unrelieved emotional distress or disturbed personality, which might demonstrate a need for professional help.

At a meeting before the pilot scheme began one group discussion centred on the distractibility and short attention span of children, which might prove to be a limiting factor in bibliotherapy. The parents of seven bereaved children and two social workers requested an analysis of a book to indicate the features that would hold a child's interest.

My choice, supported by votes from ten children aged nine to fourteen, is based on the identification of many references to typical thoughts and feelings expressed by grieving children, each instance woven naturally and sensitively into narrative and dialogue. References to bereavement in *Squib* are subtle but have proved recognisable to bereaved children who have experienced similar emotions. There are neither descriptions of death nor overt expressions of grief that could cause distress to the reader.

Nevertheless, no matter how many relevant grief symptoms and signs may be recognised in a book, that book will have little bibliotherapeutic potential unless the child is aroused by a strong storyline, presented in a stimulating style with believable characterisation and true-to-life dialogue. Because the mode of bibliotherapy considered in this study, as an art, is essentially non-directive (as outlined in Chapter 1, p.17) it is necessary both to review any proposed book as a worthwhile item of children's literature and to identify relevant aspects of grieving before recommending it.

In the following pages I set out to support my choice of *Squib*, bearing in mind the cluster of problems regarding bereaved child-readers and the bereaved children's suggestions for the choice of book. As indicated in Chapter 4 (p.41) I consider Nina Bawden's authorial approach, her style of writing, choice of situations and events, discourse, vocabulary and general presentation as eminently suitable for bereaved children.

Synopsis

Bawden follows a more or less conventional children's story pattern. A problem is identified by children, there is a 'villain', conflicts and challenges arise during the children's adventures in solving the mystery, mostly without adult intervention, and there is a satisfying outcome, although in this book perhaps not the most predictable one. The basic theme concerns the plight of an abused child. Within the first page the dilemma at the core of the story is made obvious by implication – that the identity of the eight-year-old child, Squib, and the reasons for his strange appearance and behaviour, will be sought and revealed.

Setting and plot

Set in the suburbs of a seaside city, Bawden's story contains plenty of action and is episodic in presentation. The basic outline plot is simple: four children are determined to solve the mystery of the strange child, nicknamed 'Squib', whom they observe at a park playground. Kate, aged eleven, thinks he may be her younger brother whose body was never recovered from the sea after a swimming disaster. Problems and crises hinder the progress of their quest of search and rescue. For a sequence of plot events see Figure 6.1. *Outline of Plot* (p.93).

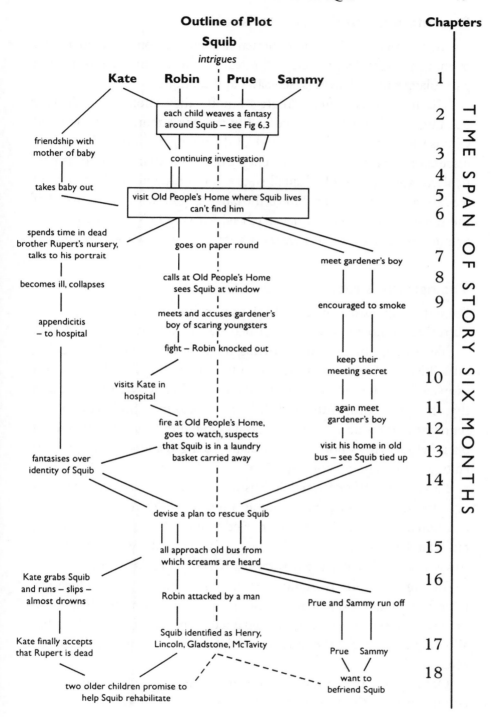

Figure 6.1 Outline of plot

Presentation and the narrator's role

Bawden initially makes few experiential demands on her readers, the opening paragraphs projecting the reader into a familiar setting of a park playground of swings, see-saws and sandpit.

'His name was Squib..."there's Squib," they shouted.' (p.7) This opening line immediately focuses the reader's attention on the child who is the pivot of the story. Three of the younger child readers in our discussion regarded the author's choice of the nickname 'Squib' as particularly apt for a child of small stature, but only one of the ten child readers, a boy of fourteen, linked the name 'Squib' with the firework of the same name. '"You can never tell which way he's going to jump," Sammy explained, "he just whizzes about like a firework."' (p.7)

The narrator's role

Presenting the story in the third person, the narrator occupies an obtrusive 'companion' role, described by one ten-year-old reader as, '...like a friend by my side, showing me and telling me what's going on.' This remark echoes Tucker's opinion, attributing Bawden's success as an author to her skill in getting close to a child's eye view of events, in that she can '...deal with childish fantasies within a child-centred presentation...the success of her books suggests that this theme of personal growth is popular with many young readers so long as it is embedded in a good story' (p.151).

Bawden herself explained, in Blishen (1975), 'I wanted to write, not as a grown-up looking back, but as a former child, remembering the emotional landscape I had once moved in, how I felt, what concerned me, what I wanted to know...because I remembered my own childhood so vividly, particularly the frustration of being a child' (p.62).

Taking this role as omniscient author/narrator can produce the richest of all narrational contribution: that of providing the reader not only with observations of setting, characters and general story-line, but allowing insight into the thoughts and innermost feelings of the characters.

Occasionally the narrational persona changes. Bawden shifts her relationship with the reader from narrator to an authorial voice, using asides. As narrator she describes Squib as 'Always alone, and lonely looking too,' and then adds, 'which is not quite the same' (p.7). She also slips in the occasional didacticism: 'She spat out one word, "procrastinator." "What's that?" Sammy asked, liking the sound of this. "Putting off till tomorrow what you could do today"' (p.98).

Bawden introduces 'good' and 'bad' characters, but there is no direct moralising in the narrative. Moral issues are raised, mostly through dialogue, and the reader is given freedom to ponder on such comments as – 'Kate drew a deep breath. "Tying a little boy up like a dog! It's the most frightful thing"' (p.18). Intrigued to know why Nina Bawden had chosen the topic of child cruelty as a theme for a children's novel, I wrote to her. In her reply she explained that she knew of a court case concerning a small boy who had been tethered to a shed by a collar and chain. Neighbouring children had seen the situation, woven a story around the child and had not reported the matter for several days.

Again, the authorial voice, through the narrator, guides and may influence the reader as, whilst condemning the cruelty meted out to Squib, she rationalises the situation, implying that the cook-house-keeper's behaviour could be the unfortunate product of her life situation. The woman had no option but to take on the care of the child when relations were killed and then return to her thug of a husband after losing her job. Two girl readers singled out the following passage for comment, saying that they needed to stop and think about the meaning, which might cause them to reconsider their initial denunciation of the woman. '"She meant to be kind, perhaps... She wasn't used to children, she'd never had any of her own. She kept him clean and fed but she treated him like a puppy, shutting him up to stop him being a nuisance."' (Spoken by Kate's mother, p.122.)

Characterisation

Comprehensive biographies of most characters, both protagonist and subsidiary roles, are provided. Within the first chapter the reader is introduced to the four main characters including Squib: Kate, eleven years old, now an only child since her brother disappeared, presumed drowned, Kate's friend Robin, aged twelve, his five-year-old brother Sammy, and his seven-year-old sister Prue, with details of their physical

appearance, nature, temperament, interaction with other people, inter-
dependence with each other and their response to various events in
their lives (see Figure 6.2 *The Child Characters in Squib*, p.97).

I use the word 'introduced' deliberately because as the story unfolds
Bawden reveals further details of each character. Initially there is no
overall description of Squib, yet there is sufficient to intrigue the reader,
'…a small pale child, pale-skinned, pale-haired' (p.7), the repetition of
'pale' reinforcing the image of the pathetic child. A reader is able to
build up a physical image of Squib. Over several chapters Bawden
gradually adds snippets of detail, mostly reinforcing the inital impression of weakness and 'paleness', likening his thick pale lashes to a
curtain and his face to a pale flower. Throughout the story Squib's frailty
is emphasised. Descriptions are inventive yet realistic and easily imagin-
able. When Kate is attending to a cut on Squib's leg, she feels the leg
might snap like a twig if she handles it roughly. We are told that when
Robin, the elder boy, picks Squib up, 'He felt horribly light – all bones,
Robin thought, like a big dead bird he'd once found on a beach' (p.110).
Mostly through dialogue, the reader gains an insight into each child's
mind, except for that of Squib who neither speaks nor is credited with
any thoughts, perceptions or aspirations throughout the whole story.
Withholding this information adds impact to the mystery as almost
every other character, main or subsidiary, is granted voiced or indirectly
voiced opinions.

Bawden's main modes of character presentation, through dialogue
and narrative, are discussed later under the sections concerning **style**
and **readability**.

Reader response

Children build up unique images of a story that may bear limited resemblance to the author's visualisation. As Iser (1978) explains, 'the reader,
however, can never learn from the text how accurate or inaccurate are
his views of it' (p.166). Iser contends that this fundamental asymmetry
between writer and reader is essentially functional in the interaction
between text and reader, 'giving rise to communication in the reading
process' (p.167).

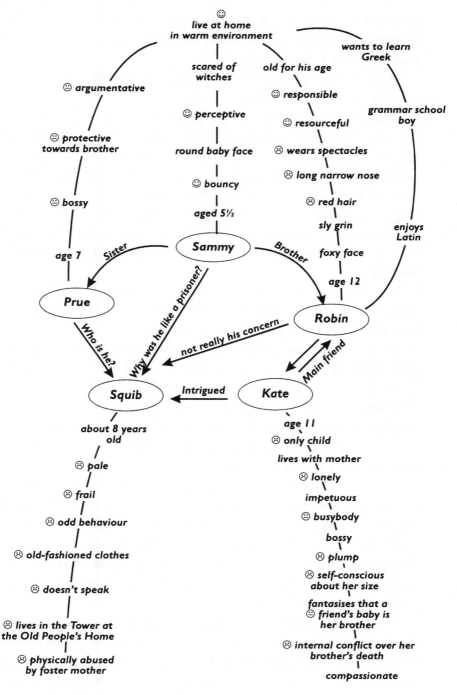

Figure 6.2 The child characters in 'Squib'

The reader's response involvement in actualising the text can be manipulated by switching perspectives. This occurs within and between chapters in *Squib* causing the reader to create missing parts of the story from what Iser refers to as '**gaps**'.

Most of the chapters in *Squib* are satisfyingly complete in themselves, few merging into subsequent chapters.

One child reader, obviously recognising such gaps when asked if she read the whole book straight through, replied, 'No, I felt I wanted to stop at the end of some chapters to think what had just happened and what might happen next; that's what the person who was telling me the story meant me to do, wasn't it?' Her curiosity and interest had challenged her to pause in her reading, to consolidate text previously read, and draw on her own experiential bank to imagine and create parts of the story not in the actual text, thus enhancing the story far beyond her reading.

It is no wonder that Crago (1983) related in his book *Prelude to Literacy* how they even *taught* their child Anna to speculate about fictional gaps from the early age of three.

Chambers, in Hunt (1990), refers to two types of gaps, a **superficial gap** where the author leaves out what he or she expects the child to know already, and **deeper** gaps which challenge the reader to shift his focus and contribute to the story, the success of which is dependent on whether the child accepts that challenge. The child who does recognise and is able to fill those gaps has an enhanced read, yet, as in *Squib*, the story proves fulfilling as it stands.

Chambers identifies various categories of gap. A **gap of situation** occurs when Kate had been thinking about her brother. '...she thought, Suppose, suppose...' (p.28). Here the question of whether Squib could possibly be Rupert is raised again and left open-ended, a quietly contemplative chapter ending for the reader. This proves to be a **temporary gap**, not being closed until the end of the story when Squib's real identity is revealed.

The ending of Chapter 10 leaves a **permanent gap** concerning Rupert's fate. 'Or perhaps he had been washed up on some foreign shore...' (p.76) A **complete gap** throughout the entire story, that of Squib's ability to talk, has no completion; it is a **complete blank**.

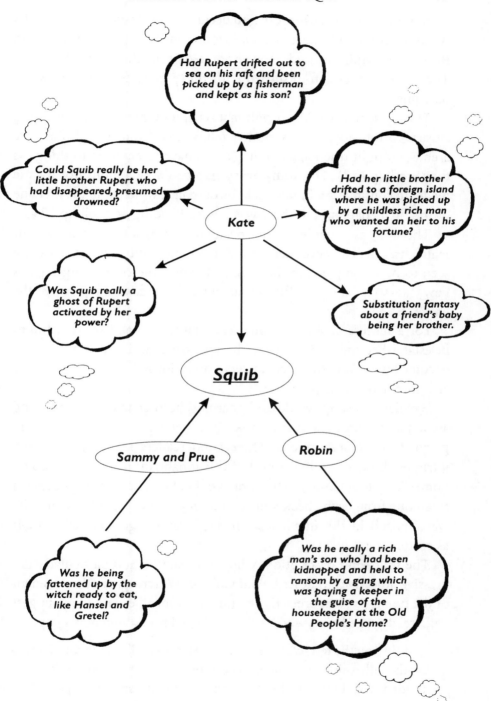

Figure 6.3 The child characters' fantasies

A more urgent **incomplete gap** occurs in the closure of Chapter 13 when the children suspect that Squib is in some immediate danger, '"Oh Robin, it's awful," she said, "You've got to do something quick!"' (p.97). The reader is then left in suspense for thirty more pages to know the outcome.

The last sentence of the penultimate chapter suggests an unsatisfying closure to the story, Kate's mother telling her, '"But in real life there aren't any right true happy endings. You have to get used to things as they are."' (p.123). This **temporary gap** could be a motivator for the reader to continue reading to seek the outcome, which is, in the first line of the final chapter, 'But there was a happy ending after all' (p.124).

The story as a whole can be considered **complete**, in that the four main characters achieve their goal in rescuing Squib, but it can also be seen to be incomplete, in that a sequel is possible concerning Squib's new life-style and his further activities and adventures with the children.

For a successful author–reader communication and relationship to be established the reader needs to be able to empathise within the story, become involved with the characters, cope with switches of perspective and complete any gaps.

Bawden's descriptive skills concerning both characters and setting are apparent throughout the book. Even her secondary characters are given detailed descriptions. Three child readers in our group were intrigued by her vivid portrayal of this inhabitant of the old people's home: 'The flesh hung from the bones of her face in powdery pouches, a small one from each cheek and several bigger ones from her chin. She was almost bald; the little hair she had left was orange coloured and soft as cotton wool' (p.44).

The following description, which uses similes and particularly ex-pressive adjectives to describe old Colonel Wittering, another resident of the home, drew appreciative comments from all except the youngest child reader, aged nine, who '...didn't like to know about ugly people'.

> ...sitting on the terrace, eyes blinkered like an owl's in the sun. Old hands with veins like tender, blue ropes and a thick nose with a divided red blob at the tip...and laughed, showing jagged mustard-yellow teeth with a flash of gold at the back. (p.65)

One adult reader objected to these descriptions, regarding them as crude and unsuitable for children. It can be appreciated that this adult was speaking with his own image interpretation of the text, based on his own visual experience, but it is highly unlikely that a child would conjure up a similarly gruesome image. One child might imagine a very basic character image of the old person, merely using what he gleans from the actual text. Another, using his imaginative and experiential bank, may amplify the textual details to include a voice, clothing or mannerisms. Most children today are bombarded with visual and aural stimuli from TV, video and films and build up vast memory banks from which they can create their own images, though these may bear limited resemblance to the author's visualisation. Nevertheless, as Iser (1978) explains, 'The reader, however, can never learn from the text how accurate or inaccurate are his views of it' (p.166). Iser contends that this fundamental asymmetry between writer and reader is essentially functional in the interaction between text and reader, '...giving rise to communication in the reading process' (p.167).

Bawden's writing at varying levels caters for different interpretations according to the reader's knowledge and experience, one example being, 'As they came near she smiled with one side of her mouth...she spoke out of the side of her mouth too' (p.44). Only the child reader who was aware of the after-effects of a stroke could really understand the relevance of this passage.

Readability

Squib could be described as an easy read, confirmed by all the ten children asked to voice their opinions. Although at first glance it may appear that Bawden writes in a childish way, her language is simple yet sophisticated. There are relatively few words of more than two syllables and sentences are mostly short, of an average of ten to eleven words. Longer sentences are well divided by commas and semicolons. A child with a reading age of ten could read and understand these everyday words without difficulty.

Both narrative and dialogue are alive with interest and detail. It can be seen from the analysis of a passage of just four sentences totalling 189 words, how much detail is presented, producing such a comprehensive description of the scene that little further imagination is required. (See page 16 in *Squib* and extract on p.127. Bawden informs me that this passage probably appears particularly vivid as it describes an actual place which, had she discovered it as a child, she would have explored with delight.)

It could be claimed that Bawden's writing meets the term 'a nourishing language' coined by Jones and Buttrey (1970), referring to a book which is easy to understand, imbibe and digest, evokes intense interest with a concentrated yet fluid description and provides plenty of text for imaginative minds (nourishing). Bawden's style in *Squib* also meets Tucker's (1981) argument that children usually seem to prefer a style that does not present too many difficulties, uses a high percentage of direct speech and a less complex vocabulary. He does, however, acknowledge that children, '...respond imaginatively to the **sound** of words as opposed to their content – probably the single most unpredictable topic to try to understand in the whole field of children's literature' (p.13). White, quoted in Hunt (1991), argues that children love words which give them a hard time, provided they are '...in a context which absorbs their attention' (p.104). Fisk, in Blishen (1975), confirms this notion, 'Words – even if only partly understood create atmosphere, sensation, magic and so on' (p.121). Blishen (1975) agrees, 'Words in themselves are such a pleasure to children' (p.148).

The two previous remarks are echoed by one child reader who, having enjoyed the story of *Squib*, appeared particularly thrilled by finding, as she expressed it, 'five five-finger words and one six-finger word'. She was referring to the number of syllables: *cornucopia* (p.58), *indescribable* (p.110), *refrigerator* (p.24), *indecisively* (p.43), *procrastinator* (p.98), all of five syllables and *inconspicuously* (p.56), of six syllables. (This child, aged ten, did not even know the meanings of four of the words!)

This child's pleasurable find would appear to confirm Hunt's (1991) remark that '...some writers deliberately avoid using words they think the child doesn't know and this emasculates the prose' (p.104).

Bawden's use of speech and dialogue

Three child readers expressed a preference for *Squib*, in which Bawden uses a wealth of dialogue serving various functions, rather than *Bridge To Terabithia*, Paterson (1977), written for a similar age group, in which the story-telling is predominantly narrative.

In *Squib* eleven out of eighteen chapters open with **direct speech** (see pp.129–30). Direct speech tends to draw the reader closer to the narrator, immediately focusing the reader's attention. This fact drew recognition and appreciation from a twelve-year-old boy suffering from reduced concentration span. He remarked, 'If someone in a book is talking to me I listen. I kept losing the story in *Bridge to Terabithia* because the storyteller could have been telling anyone, not me. I didn't get to know the characters.' (None of the chapters opens with direct speech.)

In at least nine instances in *Squib* Bawden creates impact by using short narrative sentences of three to four words following dialogue. This allows the reader the opportunity to reflect on the given statement, as in the example '...and a bit thinner it could *be* him, couldn't it? Robin thought he understood.' (p.31)

Bawden uses **direct speech** to add details to her characters. Her readers are invited to Prue's home to eavesdrop on her mother's comment about her disobedience, '"Prue wouldn't listen to God Almighty," said Mrs Tite.' (p.38)

Bawden also uses **indirect speech**. Focusing on Robin as he is watching Kate, she comments, 'His mother said that girl [Kate] needs her corners knocked off' (p.10). When Bawden wants to infer that the two younger children would be very interested in Squib because he looks vulnerable, she uses direct description in narrative to identify one facet of their characters. 'Sammy and Prue always chose friends they could order about...both so bossy and bouncy...' (p.8).

In Bawden's use of **reported thought** in a narrative passage we learn more about both Kate and Robin. 'Kate...liked to get to the bottom of things. Nothing else to occupy her mind, Robin thought, feeling a bit sour.' (p.8)

Bawden uses **free direct speech** (no intermediary narrator) together with a lexis readily recognisable at child level **to give impetus**, as seen in the quick-fire repartee between Robin and his sister Prue.

'Don't do that!'

'I can't help it. I got air inside me.'

'Keep it to yourself then.'

'I can't, you get air inside you, it has to come out, that's Nature. If I tried to keep it back I might die.'

'Perhaps we'd all rather you took the chance!' (pp.36–37)

Bawden also uses dialogue to create **atmosphere and tension** without the need for back-up narrative description, as in this simple, single utterance, '"You know, we might have been burned in our beds. Burned alive!"' (p.81)

Robin's mother describes Rupert's disappearance and his father's death in a 161-word speech **to bring in knowledge of past events** which adds to the depth of the story. (pp.37–38) Direct speech can **express intense emotion**, as when Kate thought she was going to drown and suffered a flashback to the previous tragedy. 'She gasped, "Get Rupert, not me."' (p.117)

Bawden also uses direct speech **to progress the story**. Chapter 8 ends as Kate faints. Chapter 9 is concerned with other matters. Chapter 10 begins with '"No visitor this afternoon?" Sister said.' This one sentence advances the story to a new scene, allowing the reader to fill in the narrative gap. The function of **dialect and idiolect** which can only be expressed in **direct speech** can be used to **individualise** a character who uses incorrect grammar or inappropriate words. The lower social class of the garden boy is highlighted in this sentence, '"I got chucked out last week 'cause me bike's broke."' (p.48)

Three of the older child readers commented on Bawden's use of varying positions of locutionary (spoken) and reporting clauses adding impact throughout the book. At the opening of Chapter 4 in *Squib* there is no reporting clause, '"Hey, Robin."' Chapter 8 opens with the reporting clause first, 'Kate called, "Sophie."' Chapter 13 shows an inversion whereby the locutionary clause precedes the reporting clause. '"Someone must know her name," Kate said.' (Further examples on p.129)

Bawden appears to prefer 'said' plus an adverb or adverbial phrase rather than a directly tagged reporting phrase as in 'She said sternly...' (p.42) or using a medial qualifying phrase as in, '"Oh, Robin," she said in a delighted voice, "Come and look!"' (p.78).

References are provided in a register of language readily recognised and enjoyed by children. When Robin meets the boy who was annoying the younger children he threatens, '"You rotten stinking bully, you do that again and I'll bash you good and proper"' (p.70).

She uses appropriate metaphors: – '...little men with hob-nailed boots stamped about inside her skull' (p.5), referring to a throbbing head. Some descriptions are enhanced by similes such as, '[houses]... built in pairs like Siamese twins' (p.65). Tucker (1981) emphasises Bawden's skill in getting close to a child's-eye view of events, remarking that she can '...deal with childish fantasies within a child-centred presentation...the success of her books suggests that this theme of personal growth is popular with many young readers so long as it is embedded in a good story' (p.151).

The book *Squib* and the bereaved child

Squib could be said to have a gentle, mild approach to the problems confronting a bereaved child, problems which, as we shall note in the recorded responses of ten child readers (at the end of this chapter), are recognisable only to a child who has experienced a bereavement.

Kate said of herself, '"I feel awful. All the time. Mixed up in my stomach and mixed up in my head."' In real life others often don't know how to reply to comments like that. Bawden describes Robin, 'He didn't know how to reply to that. To hide his embarrassment, he swung on the gate, lifting his feet backwards and hanging from his armpits.'

Aspects concerning bereavement expressed in *Squib*

Reluctance to mention name of deceased for fear of upsetting others

On page 26 Kate referred to Squib as, '"...about the same age as Rupert would be now..." She swallowed hard; mentioning her brother's name gave her butterflies in her stomach.'

Bewilderment at attitude of adults

'"Rupert would have been eight this September." Mrs Pollack spoke in a bright practical voice as if she were discussing a stranger. She then promptly changed the subject.' (p.26)

Refusal to accept death

Kate did have a reason to deny Rupert's death: his body had never been found although her father's had been washed up on the beach. Squib looked the same age as Rupert would have been and his eyes were almost identical to Rupert's, one eye blue and the other brown. Kate looked for support and reassurance from Robin, hoping perhaps that he would confirm her doubts.

Feelings of being unwanted or a nuisance

Two bereaved children recognised the situation of Kate's rebuff from her mother. 'Unless Kate was actually posing it bothered her mother to have her there…Kate understood this but sometimes it made her feel lonely.' (p.27) In the whole book there are only two short dialogues between Kate and her mother, one in chapter 3 and another in the penultimate chapter. Parents who have lost a child or a partner may dwell on their own personal loss or immerse themselves in an activity to the exclusion of remaining siblings.

Feeling of loss, isolation and loneliness

'She felt lonely now, more so than usual; it was thinking about Rupert, perhaps.' (p.27)

Communication with the deceased

It is quite common for bereaved people to enter a deceased person's room to feel near to that person. We read that, 'Kate then went into Rupert's room, wound the cuckoo clock and waited for the cuckoo to pop out'. Children also talk to photographs and even toys. On page 27 we read, 'Looking at his portrait, she whispered "Hallo" and moved a little to the right, to make his eyes follow her. They did, and she smiled. She said, "Hallo, Rupert."' To read about a character doing just this might prove comforting and reassure the child reader that this is normal. These are also examples of a character needing spiritual contact with the deceased.

Fantasising

As mentioned before in this chapter, each child in the story weaves a fantasy around Squib. Kate extends her fantasies to include a rich man in a yacht who, being childless, wants someone to whom he can leave his fortune. Robin gives a typical answer to an expression of fantasy of that type, "'All that silly nonsense!'" (p.94) To read about another fantasiser, albeit a fictional character, could give an 'it's all right' message to a child.

Feeling of guilt

Many children feel guilty that they may have precipitated a death, a feeling which is very real to the child but seldom understood by adults. These feelings tend to recur in times of stress, in dreams or illness, as they do for Kate who, feeling low after she has had her appendix removed, '…heard her mother's voice, in her head, "*Oh, Kate, if only you hadn't gone in the sea without telling me…*"' (p.75).

As often happens in reality, Bawden then lets her character drift off into a positive fantasy, Kate thinking of her brother drifting out to sea, not scared at all, expecting to be rescued.

Reliving the happening of a tragedy

This is also quite common in children who have witnessed or been involved in a fatal accident and again emerges in times of stress or a similar situation. Bawden describes this phenomenon so dramatically in one scene that she could have been recounting a personal experience. Kate is in danger of drowning when a life-saver tells her to put her hand on the rescuer's shoulder. 'But she couldn't. Didn't want to. And not just because she was so tired. If he [Squib] was going to drown, she wanted to drown too.' (p.117)

Nightmares

Some children fear recurring nightmares based on the scene of tragedy though not reliving the actual occurrence. Kate tells Robin about her nightmares, '"He's [Rupert] running away through a wood towards something dangerous and sometimes I can see him and sometimes I can't, but I can hear him crying. And sometimes he's drowning…"' The account goes on as Kate tells of, '"A sort of lake, deep and dark. Not like anywhere I've been. Black water…"' The colour came and went in her face and she shivered.' (p.52)

This sort of dream, so real to a child, is unfortunately too frequently pooh-poohed by adults in the close family, possibly through embarrassment.

This is where a bibliotherapist could help by projection in discussing how the character Kate was feeling, not directly addressing the child reader.

Irrational thoughts

Kate, still seeing Squib as her actual, or reincarnated, brother, attributes his disappearance for over a week to his reaction to her interfering in his life. '"It's just I keep thinking. It's since I recognised him. As if he'd been waiting for that, and as soon as I did he went away."' (p.51)

Bereavement, particularly of a sibling, can bring about similar thoughts, in an attempt to rationalise a real or imagined situation.

Confrontation with the truth

'"Rupert is dead, my darling."' Kate reacted to her mother's statement as many children do when their daydreams and wishful thinking about a dead person are challenged. 'She said a bit crossly, "Oh, I know that. I knew it all the time, really."' (p.121)

Retreat into self

Trying to persuade an apathetic bereaved person, child or adult, to get out and about is a very common problem. '"Oh, do come on, Kate, don't be so broody. It'll take you out of yourself," urged Robin.' (p.125)

Kate's answer is typical of many bereaved children, preferring to stay in their own safe environment.'"I want to stay inside myself, thank you very much... It's the most comfortable place to be."' (p.126)

Another 'retreat' aspect was recognised by one bereaved child reader when she read that Robin took off his spectacles to blot out the world. She said she used to blur her focus in similar situations.

Letting go

Perhaps the most difficult stage in grieving is finally to say 'goodbye' to the deceased person. In the story Kate spends four years grieving for her brother. The turning point comes when she is asked to help Squib's carer look after him. Bawden describes this crucial time with deep insight.

'Kate nodded. The knots inside her were loosening and she felt weak and floppy, but so happy...she touched Squib's knee with one cautious finger. She said, "Hallo, there." Minutes later she looked into his eyes, one blue eye, one brown, steadily staring. She said, "Hallo, Squib,"' (p.127).

– the moment of relinquishment at last.

Children's responses to *Squib*

Ten children (six non-bereaved) within the age range (10–14 years) for which *Squib* is recommended in the Children's Book League and Cruse Bereavement Care book lists agreed to participate in reviewing *Squib*.

Each child was asked to give his or her opinion of the book, written or tape-recorded. If necessary prompt questions were asked:

- Did you read the book straight through all at one time?
- Who did you feel was telling the story?
- Tell me about the characters.
- Do you think that the story was true to life?
- How did you feel when you were reading the story?
- Is there anything else you would like to comment on?

It was not feasible, for reasons of sensitivity and confidentiality, to provide matched samples of similar aged bereaved and non-bereaved children. Although the bereaved children, at the time of reading, were now older than the character Kate in the story, they would have been approximately her age when they were confronting their bereavement. At least two years had passed since these children had been bereaved. Parental permission was obtained and readers were informed that they might find some parts of the book distressing. All names have been changed and all tape-recordings destroyed. The children have read and agreed to their responses being seen by other people.

All the children found the book absorbing, most noticing Bawden's skill of narrative and dialogue, particularly her deep and accurate insight into children's minds. Appreciative comments were made about the real-life characters, events and particularly the amount of dialogue. The inclusion of children's recognisable bad habits and rudeness in the story appealed to the readers' sense of reality. Singled out for comment was the passage from Chapter 9 where Robin thumbs his nose at a house where he delivers newspapers, '"Want to make something of it!" he said aloud…' (p.64) Most children recognised Robin's brotherly commitment to caring for his younger siblings but were critical of the wisdom of exposing them to frightening events. Appreciation was voiced at the portrayal of unfeeling adult characters who fail to realise how adverse comments can cause long-term hurt to children. Three readers commented that adults *should* read the book to grasp that very aspect.

All appreciated the detailed descriptions accorded to the secondary characters and their activities. It is probably a compliment to Nina Bawden's writing talent that the readers felt they did not need pictures. (Two children completely failed to notice the three pen and ink drawings, described on the dust cover as 'Shirley Hughes' atmospheric illustrations'.)

The children commented on various moral issues, including Kate's lies in her fantasising about the baby being her little brother, the potential danger of allowing small children out on their own in the sea and also the ill-treatment of Squib.

Not one of the non-bereaved children recognised the subtle references to bereavement and the subsequent emotional effects. Only two of the bereaved children had received counselling, taken part in group discussions or bibliotherapy, yet they all recognised the hidden depths of meaning pertaining to bereavement. Each child tended to relate Kate's situation to his/her own experience, now seen from a therapeutic distance. Again they praised the writer for her sensitive insight into the anxieties of bereaved children. One non-bereaved child remarked that the references should have been more overt to alert other children to aspects of the grieving process.

Six children asked to retain the book for re-reading.

Responses by children who read *Squib* (taken from tape-recordings)

Children who had not been bereaved
Peter, aged 12

I thought at first that this book was too babyish for me but eventually I found out that Robin was a grammar-school boy so then I went back to the beginning and started again and began to enjoy it. I feel I'm watching things happen and someone's telling me all the details in my ear. I'm sort of with someone but I don't know who it is. There are many characters in the story, perhaps too many to remember who they really are and what they are doing there but they all fitted in, though, and I felt as if I had met them. I knew what they looked like and how they spoke to the children, Yes, the people were quite real, the children behaved like children do – it could all have happened, I suppose. Lots of scenes were described, like the playground, then where the old people lived, there was a lot on that, real spooky, and the quarry and the caravan site and that poor little Sammy, they did tease him and the old lady frightened him as well, he really seemed to believe that the witch was going to eat Squib and perhaps him too. Bet he had nightmares about that, I would have done at that age. What I thought was funny was about the baby's ear, soft and curly. It was a sad story but then life is sad sometimes.

Joseph, aged 13

I liked Robin, he had a good head on his shoulders, in fact I think he should have told the story instead of whoever it was. He was sensible and brave, but he did cry and he was in the grammar school. The characters? Rather a lot, I thought although they did all belong to make it quite a real story and real places. Somehow I felt that the book was written for younger children although the main characters were eleven and twelve. Why did they have to drag those little ones around with them? They got quite frightened some of the time. No, I didn't read the book all at once because it didn't need to be read all at once, the chapters didn't follow on so I could stop anywhere – quite a good idea really. Yes, it was true to life, particularly in some things that the children did – I don't like to say this, but the bit about belching – what a strange thing to put in a book, but that and other things like Robin putting his thumb to his nose, that's what makes it a real book. The author wasn't scared to tell the truth.

Janey, aged 10

Well, at first I thought I would like to have been Kate but I'm glad I'm not like her. She worried me – she had some silly thoughts about her little brother, talking to his picture. I like taking babies out but I would never pretend any was my brother or sister. I liked to read about all the people in the story – there were lots of them and it made the story seem real and the children did things which children do really, it's odd to put them in a book but I liked that. I thought there were some creepy bits which frightened me so I stopped reading the book when I went to bed. It took me a week to read it all. Yes, I did remember from one time to the next. It was a good story because it went to lots of different places and did lots of different adventures. Now I know it had a happy ending I'd like to read it all over again.

Pat (girl), aged 11

It's a weird story but I had to go on reading fast. I didn't stop until I'd finished. It is weird and eerie too. I liked the people in the story because they were like real people and the children were normal too, they had ordinary thoughts like I have and did things without thinking of what might happen if their parents found out. Grown-ups were ordinary too. Some were horrible like the nasty woman who had poor little Squib in her clutches and some were kind like Robin's mother and some were just interesting like the old folk and the boy in the garden. I can remember them all because they were all part of the story. It is a good book and I'd read it again and still enjoy it. Pictures? I didn't see any pictures. Well, the story didn't need any pictures to my mind because the words made my pictures, perhaps that's why I didn't notice any.

Shaun, aged 13

Well, I enjoyed the book. It's not one I would have chosen if you hadn't asked me to read it. I read the blurb on the cover and thought it was a girl's book and certainly for younger children. I'll read it again now that I know that Robin is about the same age as I am. He was very good to his little brother and sister taking them along on their adventures but I thought he might have taken greater care of them and not let them go exploring on their own. Who's telling the story? Well, I've not thought of that. I was there, sort of. When Kate and the others were talking then I'm watching and listening but when they are not talking...there's someone else telling me and describing what's going on, perhaps to anyone who's listening and sometimes just talking to me and saying things I know about so that I feel I'm their mate or something like that. I was a bit surprised, or do I mean shocked, when the author told of habits my mother would call rude but again that sort of thing is reality. In a way it reminded me of those *Famous Five* books I used to read years ago because the children were trying to solve a mystery by themselves but those stories were not real or true to life and this one is...it's similar in a way, having children solving a mystery, but again I say this one could really have happened and all the characters reminded me of someone I know, they were ordinary yet not ordinary meaning dull. Pictures? I don't look at pictures, I like to make my own pictures in my head. I don't like TV programmes made of stories I've read because their people and places are never the same as I have imagined. How did I feel? All sorts of emotions I suppose. I felt sad that any child could have been treated like that, but of course they are. I felt annoyed with the older children when they didn't look after the little ones properly. Those little children shouldn't have been allowed to go out on their own, awful things happen to children these days. They might have been murdered! They took them to places where they would be frightened and even said things to scare them. I felt angry about the man and woman who had ill-treated Squib and hoped to read of their sentence in the court but that wasn't in the book. I was relieved when Squib was fostered out with really kind loving people.

Maryanne, aged 11

It's a good story and could be real, but it's a bit gloomy and sad in places and I think you'd have to be in a happy mood to read it or you would be crying over that little stick of a boy and his bruises. I would never have picked a book with a dead boy in it, particularly if he was a ghost. I thought Kate was lovely but she was really lonely at home. Her mother didn't seem to bother with her very much...it was a good thing she had the two other families to make her welcome and include her in what they were doing. She shouldn't have romanced about that baby being hers. My mother says I romance about things which I don't have but I don't do any harm, neither did Kate really. I don't really feel anyone telling the story. I'm just there, watching and feeling it all. Sometimes I want to shout, 'Don't do it!' or 'Don't go!' especially when Kate went into the quarry lake after Squib. Why did the author put that bit in? It got me all het up thinking *she* might drown. Yes, there were lots of other people in the book. Why? Well, it made it all more real to me, it felt like a real place with all sorts of people doing all sorts of things like they do in real life. I think I'll find another book by the same author. She knows about what children think and do so they must be good books.

Sarah, aged 19

Sarah, an emotionally disturbed girl, but not from bereavement, noticed the book and when told what it was about asked to read it. I thought it would be interesting to note her reaction. Sarah identified with Kate, not as a character taking part in a plot but as a child, focusing on her troubled mind and the resolving of her emotional problems, although she regarded most of the other activities as irrelevant.

> Well, that girl was all mixed up, wasn't she? She took a whole book to sort herself out. Still, I wouldn't mind if I could have a whole book to sort myself out but perhaps I'd have to have things happen to me too…it was worth it in the end. Poor little chap! Yes, there were other people in the story but what did they have to do with what Kate had to sort out? And what about those 'wrinklies'? Who wants them in a book – ugh! And that wild boy? And the baby's family, none of them were part of the real story.

Children who had been bereaved

Michelle, aged 15
(She was 9 when her brother, Peter, died as a result of a prank)

> I thought the story realistic as if it was being told by a child, because of the insight, yet a child wouldn't have the ability to set down those thoughts in suitable prose. Kate's mother wasn't much help, always doing her own thing…or maybe, being an artist, she was too emotional to discuss things. I wonder if she might still be hoping that Rupert had not really drowned, because she drew Squib in Rupert's image. That's just a thought, it wasn't in the book. Quite a few mixed-up people in the story, not a very happy or contented selection, rather crowded, really, but she [Nina Bawden] did take us off on another track away from the main story from time to time. I think that showed the reader that everyone has a life split into various parts. I don't see why those little children were involved in the solving of the mystery, they were frightened and they didn't understand really. I wonder if the author had had something like that happen to her. She knew how it felt when she told of Kate being there when Rupert disappeared and she had guilty feelings when her mother told her she should have watched him more

carefully – it made her feel guilty for ever…well…of course you know that Peter died when he fell off the park pavilion and I was there with the others laughing and cheering at him larking about. I know he was older than me and he ought to have known better but Gran and Auntie said I should have told him to come down, blaming me almost. That hurt and it still hurts. The ambulance took him away, he was actually dead then but Mum went to the hospital telling me that he would recover and for a whole week I waited for him to regain consciousness so that I could say how sorry I was, but it wasn't to be. It was the girls in school who told me that their parents had been to his funeral. I remember telling my mother that I would never believe anything she said again and I didn't speak to her for a long time. I used to have tantrums, awful ones. If anything like that happens to me I shall be honest however awful the news is. Of course they couldn't have a funeral for Rupert but there must have been one for Kate's father…maybe she wasn't allowed to go, like me, so it's not easy to let go and say goodbye then. Like Kate I used to sort of see Peter like a ghost and talk to him in private too. Kate had been four years trying to cope with Rupert's death, all on her own, too long, and then she managed to let go at last within a few months, probably because she had something positive to do in trying to solve the mystery surrounding Squib. It's a good book, easy to read and it rolled along in an exciting way. It makes you think and realise that life isn't all happiness, and when people have their secret thoughts which they can't express to anyone it's, well, sort of soothing to read about similar thoughts in a book. Like Kate, we shouldn't be sad when things don't go the way we want them – Squib was going to be happy eventually with Emerald. The story didn't really upset me but it's so true because I know now, but didn't then, that when someone dies relatives often look for someone to blame and when that person is a child then guilt can overwhelm and make the child feel unloved. I liked the book because it provided many hints which triggered off thoughts of things which perhaps needed sorting out for me. I wonder if it will help other bereaved children.

Brian, aged 14
(His grandfather died when he was 8.)

I didn't particularly want to read this book when I read the synopsis on the front cover; it looked and sounded like a girl's book. Robin was quite a thinker and showed initiative to act on his own. He was a strength to Kate and without him Squib might not even have been rescued. Although Robin remarked that it was a bit morbid to keep Rupert's room like a shrine it looked as if underneath it all he was sad when his gran threw everything out when his grandfather died...I'm talking as if Robin was a real person, he seemed real. That hit me because when Gramps died Gran kept his things around even though she knew he'd never want them again...you can't get rid of people's...what do I mean...souls or spirits? just because they've died. If people want to talk to a spirit, then why not? It seemed to give Kate some comfort. And they shouldn't be told that they are going mad. I don't think that readers who hadn't had anyone they loved die would pick out the references to bereavement. Perhaps the message should have been stronger to give more understanding to other children. Another thing, now I think of it, I can sometimes sense Gramps around, can smell his pipe and his aftershave on his coat so Kate wasn't so odd.

Nicholas, aged 13
(His father died when he was 8)

It was a very interesting book with many aspects of children's thoughts brought to life. She [Bawden] really wrote as if she knew children deeply and she wasn't too prim and proper to write expressing words and actions close to reality. She brought out several cases of parents' ignorance over just how much a child should be told and is able to understand, such as when Robin didn't know of Kate's real experiences until his mother told him and he had already made some unfortunate remarks to Kate...let me find the part I mean...here it is, page 38: 'Robin felt sick. He said, "Poor Kate, I mean she must think it was all her fault."' That ought to make the reader stop and think, or, it ought to make parents stop and think. There was another case where Kate's mother had said something about she was afraid that Kate's talents were only domestic. And another, too, when she had praised another child for being the only one with much sense and that had really hurt Kate. Plenty of food for thought for parents. I couldn't believe that Dad was dead; he was only thirty when he died; I was eight. If I hadn't seen him in his coffin and gone to the crematorium as well I might have even expected him back. Adults are a bit odd about death. My mother and the others didn't want to talk about such things to a little boy. I imagine this was the same for Kate; if she had been included in the arrangements for her father's funeral, which wasn't mentioned in the book, she might have come to terms with Rupert's presumed death. Robin wanted to talk to his mother about Kate, it's on the next page: 'He would have liked to say, "Kate thinks he's still alive," but it was not the sort of thing he could say to his mother.' (p.39) And look at this on page 37: '"Drowned." Mrs Tite lowered her voice to speak of the dead.' People whispered to each other when Dad died so that I couldn't hear and I wanted to hear. I liked the book; it was real for the most part. People do drown and are not washed up for ages, perhaps not at all. Yes, it should be written about how children feel when someone dies. This is a very mild book on that topic. Children believe what they read in books if the story seems true to life.

Cheryl, aged 14
(Her brother died, aged 4, when she was 9)

Squib's an excellent book, very touching and so true in the way the author expresses the children's emotions. It's sad but I had to read it straight through. It has, like Mrs B. says at school – momentum – so I read the whole book at once then went back to the parts which really affected me and brought back thoughts of five years ago. I did cry and I'm not afraid to admit it because Jamie too was four when he died in Great Ormond Street Hospital. I wasn't there. I didn't see him dead and I wasn't allowed to go to the funeral so in a way I was like Kate, having no definite evidence that my little brother was dead. Robin didn't agree with Rupert's room being kept like a shrine. No wonder Kate thought that he might need his room again. Well, Jamie's room was kept like that, I used to go in there and talk to his photo too, until this year when they changed it all around for Jenny [sister]. Mum and Dad cried and cried while we were putting his things away, me too. It was like sending his memory away. I think we really let him go then. Am I being sentimental when I say that his book had helped me complete my grieving? I don't think I need to cry over Jamie any more. I wish I'd read *Squib* when Jamie died then I could have cried it all out then. Sometimes, like when Jamie died, people didn't cry in front of me so I thought I shouldn't cry either and if I'd had the excuse to cry over a book it would have been better. Do you know what made me really cry this time? It was at the end when Kate said, 'Hallo, Squib.' I think that's when she really said goodbye to Rupert. And that's the real end to mourning, isn't it? And the real start to the future.

CHAPTER 7

Discussion and implications

Bibliotherapy for bereaved children using fiction literature would not be feasible unless an adequate selection of books could be identified. In this study over 70 books in current circulation, providing a wide range of references to bereavement, have been located, presenting death topics ranging from a minor mention in the stories to major themes throughout whole books. The portrayal of the intensity of emotion ranges from mere allusions to death to deeply graphical descriptions of illness, death and grief.

Whilst there has proved to be a similarity in the frequency of incidence of storyline death topics between the late nineteenth century books and those written in the late twentieth century, there is a marked difference in presentation. As described more fully in Chapter 2, presentation in nineteenth century children's stories was basically **third party narration** in **descriptive form**, usually coupled with moral or religious overtones. However, children taking part in this study were fascinated by the format and presentation of these older books.

Contemporary novels appear to meet the contemporary child, frequently through a **first-person** narrator, providing insight into children's thoughts, feelings and emotions and drawing the child reader further into recognition and identification with the characters in the book. As Nicholas Fisk, in Blishen (1975), explains, 'Book-reading children have changed from being seen and not heard, having access only to books on moral issues, to children who live amongst adults, join in their conversation, watch TV and are influenced by adverts...' (p.48).

The study has highlighted what, in my opinion, has proved to be one of the most valuable innovations in contemporary books suitable for bibliotherapy: the use of first-person child narrators. Adopting this approach the author can express thoughts, fears, emotions and opinions from a child character's point of view. This opens up unique opportunities for child readers to consider the characters' predicaments that might have a close bearing on their own situations, particularly when addressing those issues which adults tend to evade or may not even consider to be of relevance to children.

Parents' opinions are valuable

Parents of bereaved children, invited to read some of the selected books, expressed shock, astonishment and even embarrassment at the depth and range of content of some teenage novels. *The Boy in the Bubble* (Strachan 1993) contains close references to a dying teenager and sex, *Falling Apart* (Wilson 1989) details a girl's suicide attempt and *I Carried You on Eagles' Wings* (Mayfield 1990) gives a harrowing account of a death scene. A few adults commented on the 'raw' mode of presenting aspects such as terminal illness and death expressed both in narrative and emotive dialogue, some of which they considered to be brutal, undisguised and too forthright. Nevertheless, parents were in agreement that all references were within possible and acceptable normality but questioned their suitability for youngsters, being of the opinion that some of these aspects could not be discussed with children. Yet these were the very books which several teenagers singled out, finding such open and detailed descriptions refreshing, enlightening and true to life.

Children's opinions are valuable

Older teenagers in particular valued the opportunity to read and re-read full-length novels containing those aspects of death which are seldom aired openly.

Highlighted were:

- how far one can openly grieve when a loved one is dying
- apprehension when asked to view and/or touch a dead body
- discussing an anticipated death
- coping with a sudden death of a peer friend.

Two parent-bereaved seventeen-year-old boys appreciated references to openly expressed grief in male characters of their age group. Books intended for older teenagers have recently shown a tendency to be 'unisex', in that hidden and overt grief feelings are depicted in both male and female adolescent characters. However, some books do shed light on gender variations in child and teenage grief. This is evident in *We, The Haunted* (Johnson 1989), in which the two protagonists, a boy and girl in their middle teens, each narrate part of the story, giving girls an insight into boys' emotional reactions and vice versa.

Two bereaved early-teenage girl readers, having read *Your Friend Rebecca* (see Chapter 5 p.71) and identified with Rebecca's non-typical and unacceptable behaviour, remarked on this aspect, feeling relief that such behaviour was 'normal' in the circumstances.

The general consensus among teenagers was that if adults read modern children's fiction containing references to grieving children, a greater understanding would result. Youngsters could then express their grief openly. 'We're not expected to mourn, there's too much secrecy with the adults. They don't show their feelings in front of us so we daren't show ours for fear of upsetting them, yet we all go away and cry in our private places...' complained an eleven-year-old. Children pinpointed references in books concerning matters that they felt they could not discuss with their families, including peripheral matters following the loss of one parent. Mention was made of the refusal of the remaining parent to speak about the deceased person and the possibility of that parent's new relationships, as in *John's Book*. Two teenagers welcomed the inclusion of viewpoints and behaviour of bereaved adults, as described in *Two Weeks with the Queen*. Others felt that insight into communication difficulties between bereaved adults and children was particularly valuable. These further innovations, found in more recently written novels, could prove to be a valuable contribution to bereavement bibliotherapy. In the teenagers' opinion some of these selected books should be more widely read, possibly in the safe environment of school, using the book as a class reader when general free discussion could take place, not merely brought in after a bereavement. 'We'd all cope better and would know what to say to our bereaved friends,' remarked a fourteen-year-old boy.

Parents and children were agreeably surprised that the writers of the books mentioned above, along with others, showed such profound understanding of the overt expressions, behaviour and deep, hidden emotions of bereaved children. None of these books proves to be truly morbid; each tells a story of relatively normal children in a recognisable environment dealing with everyday happenings.

Without exception, each reviewed book avoided many pitfalls of young and older people when approaching a bereaved child. It is refreshing to note that there is neither slang reference to death, such as 'popped his clogs', 'snuffed it', nor euphemisms such as 'she was too good for this world', 'gone to sleep', or 'Jesus has taken her'. These latter phrases can trigger off powerful psychological responses of fear and uncertainty. Common platitudes such as 'You've still got us' or 'You'll feel better soon' did not appear in any book either. Surprisingly, the absence of such phrases, usually uttered by adults and meant in all good faith but meaning little, and often distancing children and adults, was not noticed by any adult until pointed out. This led to a requested meeting when we focused on identifying platitudes which are of no true value or could even be harmful to youngsters.

Happy endings are not necessarily the norm in present-day children's novels. In the selected books there are no miracle cures, characters do die, sometimes in horrific circumstances, young people suffer agonising reactions to bereavement with no promises of early recovery, but in each one there is some hope and comfort. Sensitive issues which most adults shirk when confronted by a grieving child are addressed realistically through good plots and lively expressive writing.

I consider that each book reviewed meets Hollindale's recommendation. In *Choosing Books for Children* (1974) he pronounces one ethical principle for children's writers, that they should not depict situations in which emotional destitution is overwhelmingly sudden or overwhelmingly complete. He writes that '...there must be enough light to steer by' (p.23).

I reiterate, the use of contemporary fiction books to help children come to terms with stressful situations in their lives is not a recent innovation. In 1971 Tod set out to explore this possibility, finding that when children could not bring themselves to discuss their own personal fears

and anxieties, they were usually willing to talk about fictional characters and events which reflected their own predicament. Addressing
thoughts and anxieties from an external viewpoint tends to lead to a
more rational outcome.

Tod stresses that a book should not be merely a vehicle for catharsis
but should provide **good reading** too. Confirmation of this aspect
comes from Cohen (1987) who, although a psychologist, also stresses
the need for a story to be positive and supportive, and above all, worth
reading. Willard, in Blishen (1975), remarks, 'Many a child will be
helped by finding his worries rationally discussed in a fictional setting'
(p.162). Tucker (1978) echoes this, recommending that, 'If he [the
reader] is undergoing stress in his personal life...and finds novels that
touch on such things...he may benefit...a phenomenon sometimes
referred to as "bibliotherapy"' (p.17).

Since the time when Tod and Tucker expressed their forward-
thinking opinions, children's authors have altered their presentation of
realism, resulting in far more appropriate material being available for
potential benefit through bibliotherapy.

Although non-directive bibliotherapy is not yet established in the
UK, there appears to be a growing interest from librarians, teachers and
counsellors in using 'ordinary' children's fiction to help bereaved
children.

The strength of using fiction lies in the fact that the child can become
his own therapist, reading and re-reading a book, perhaps discovering
new levels of meaning, interpretation, understanding and relevance to
his own situation. The very length of a book of fiction can prove to be a
point of strength in bibliotherapy, providing more scope than counselling, allowing a child to explore his feelings in his own time scale.

Books can act as a catalyst in the grieving process. They may evoke
emotional catharsis, prompting overt grief which may not have surfaced
previously. This can bring relief of negative feelings or lead to attitudi-
nal and strategy changes, all within a safe non-confrontational climate.

However, there are certain cautionary guidelines and limitations that
require consideration before recommending some of the books listed in
this study. Hollindale (1974) warned that a writer should not deprive

readers of the minimum emotional shelter that he would regard as '...needful in daily life for a child of his own' (p.23).

In Chapter 5 it has been noted that selected books are graded for depth of emotion. I would advise that discretion be exercised before selecting certain books in the **emo** (emotional) category. This selection should take into consideration the child's strengths and limitations which need to be recognised and assessed by a person who is also thoroughly conversant with the available books, their content, presentation and potential impact.

As has been demonstrated in this study, death is no longer a taboo topic in children's literature. The realistic presentation of illness, dying and death in contemporary novels presents an opportunity for bereaved and non-bereaved children to appreciate the anguish that may be involved in coming to terms with a bereavement. Realistic fiction covering a time span can place the bereaved child in a 'Janus' position, looking two ways: outwards as if through a window towards resuming normal life, but also inwards, enabling a therapeutic rationalisation process to take place.

Children's fiction of high literary value, written in the past thirty years, is readily available. These books, together with the well-known classics mentioned in Chapter 3, embrace virtually all the aspects of bereavement shown in the diagrams in Chapter 5.

I would suggest that there are specific values in introducing fiction rather than non-fiction or direct counselling:

- wide choice, availability and easy access to books
- the reading child can progress in private, reading a book at his own pace
- if the child wishes he can discuss problems through the third party of a character
- adults can find books for young children that address aspects frequently found embarrassing or too sensitive to broach personally.

At the outset of this study I found few references recommending the use of children's fiction to help bereaved children and even fewer recording the practice of bibliotherapy. In the light of the number and scope of books discovered, having noted the authors' understanding and expression of depth and delicacy in reference to bereavement and also the opinions generously offered by the children involved in this study, I consider that I now have sufficient evidence to substantiate the potential of bibliotherapy for bereaved children.

Appendix A

Analysis of passage from Squib – opening of Chapter 2

The church clock struck half past twelve as they came out of the sunlight of the little park into the green hush of the footpath that ran from the station road down to the church and the town.

(sentence 1, 38 words)

This was a busy suburb, only ten miles from the heart of the city, but the path was quiet and shaded as any country walk: no house near, only the churchyard and then the ends of gardens on one side, nettles and compost heaps, and the tall, forest trees of Turner's Tower on the other.

(sentence 2, 55 words)

Once a gentleman's mansion, the Tower was now an Old People's Home, and though part of the garden close to the house had been kept up, the rest of the grounds had run to tangle and wilderness; the fences broken, the great trees, growing unchecked, choking laurel and holly and housing grey squirrels and pigeons and jays that robbed nearby gardens in summer, and foxes that raided the dustbins in winter.

(sentence 3, 71 words)

The townspeople complained about the squirrels that stripped their raspberry canes and nibbled their crocus in bud and wrote angry letters to the local paper.

(sentence 4, 25 words)

Total 189 words: 42 two-syllable words; 3 three-syllable words.

Nouns: 42 – 31 concrete, 2 of time, 2 of sensation, 5 positional, 2 proper nouns

clock	park	house	church
churchyard	dustbins	fences	suburb
gardens	laurel	holly	nettles
city	town	path	compost heap
squirrels	walk	trees	pigeons
grounds	mansion	heart	paper
wilderness	canes	tangle	foxes
letters	townspeople	jays	footpath
crocus	ends	side	sunlight
hush	winter	summer	miles
Turner's Tower		Old People's Home	

Adjectives: 21 – 7 of state, 4 of size, 7 positional, 2 of colour, 1 of ownership.

busy	quiet	shaded	broken
in-bud	close	country	local
little	tall	old	great
forest	gentleman's	station	green
grey	church	nearby	angry
ten			

Verbs: 13 (5 with dynamic negative connotations).

choking	robbed	stripped	nibbled
complained	struck	came	kept
run	wrote	ran	growing
housing			

Adverbs: 4.

unchecked	out	down	up

Opening sentences of each chapter

Three declarative opening sentences: -

Ch.1. 'His name was Squib.' (p.7) – straight to main character.

Ch.15. 'Prue sobbed as she ran.' (p.105) – leads reader to question why?

Ch.18. 'But there was a happy ending after all.' (p.124) – a satisfying opening for a final chapter.

Four descriptive openings:

Ch.2. 'The church clock struck half past twelve as they came out of the sunlight of the little park into the green hush of the footpath that ran from the station road down to the church and the town.' (p.17) – setting the scene clearly.

Ch.3. 'Kate put the brake on the pram and went through the open front door of the cottage.' (p.21) – prompting the reader to find out why.

Ch.12. 'When Prue got to the shed, Sammy was already there, squatting on the ground beside the Wild One and rubbing two pebbles together.' (p.84)

Ch.16. 'The little boy was lying where he'd fallen, limp as a rag: that dreadful man, shouting and swaying in a sort of lumbering dance, Robin clinging to his knees.' (p.112) – a striking scene, easy to visualise.

Eleven chapters opening with speech

One without reporting phrase:

Ch.4. '"Hey, Robin."' (p.29)

Six with locutionary phrase first, name of speaker before 'said' in each case:

Ch.5. '"Should have asked her to tea," Mrs Tite said.' (p.35)

Ch.6. '"I don't want to," Sammy said.' (p.40)

Ch.10. '"No visitor this afternoon?" Sister said.' (p.71)

Ch.13. '"Someone must know her name," Kate said.' (p.93)

Ch.14. '"No point in just bursting down there," Robin said.' (p.98)

Ch.17. '"Prue is the only one of you with any sense," Mrs Pollack said.' (p.105)

Two with locutionary phrase in second position:

Ch.8. 'Kate called, "Sophie!"' (p.56)

Ch.9. 'Robin said, "Is she all right, Mum?"' (p.62)

One medial placing of reporting phrase:

Ch.7. '"I can't get anything out of them," Robin said. "They just look at each other and giggle."' (p.50)

One of direct thought:

Ch.11. '*Kidnapped*, Robin thought, lying awake in the hot night, *kidnapped and held to ransom.*' (p.77)

Appendix B

Suggested sources of books

The Young Book Trust Library
Book House
45 East Hill
Wandsworth
London SW 18 2QZ
Tel. 020 8516 2977
Fax. 020 8516 2978

The Children's Library at Young Book Trust receives a copy of every children's book published in the UK. All books are listed on a database with full bibliographic data enabling books on any topic to be supplied on request.

YBT (Young Book Trust) News – a publication issued termly – produces a selection list of books reviewed by children.

Cruse Bereavement Care
126 Sheen Road
Richmond
Surrey TW9 1UR
Cruse helpline: 0870 167 1677

Lists with basic reviews available on request – tel. 020 8939 9530

MEDITEC Medical and Nursing (Mail Order Books)
2 Pied Calf Yard
Sheep Market
Spalding
Lincolnshire PE11 1BE
Tel. 01775 711 617
Fax. 01775 711 963

Comprehensive catalogue on all medical aspects available on request.

Bibliography

Appleyard, J. A. (1991) *Becoming a Reader.* Cambridge: Cambridge University Press.

Barry, P. (1987) *Issues in Contemporary Critical Theory.* London: Macmillan.

Berg, P. J., Devlin, M. K. and Gedaly-Duff, V. (1980) 'Bibliotherapy with children experiencing loss.' *Issues in Comprehensive Pediatric Nursing 4,* 37–50.

Blishen, E. (ed) (1975) *The Thorny Paradise.* London: Kestrel Books.

Brown, E. F. (1975) *Bibliotherapy & Its Widening Application.* New Jersey: Scarecrow Press.

Chambers, A. (1973) *Introducing Books to Children.* London: Heinemann.

Chambers, A. (1979) 'The reader in the book.' *Signal 23, May,* 23.

Chambers, N. (ed) (1980) *The Signal Approach to Children's Books.* Harmondsworth: Kestrel Books.

Clarke, J. M. and Bostle, E. (eds) (1988) *Reading Therapy.* London: Library Association Publishers.

Cohen, L. J. (1987) 'Bibliotherapy: Using literature to help children deal with difficult problems.' *Journal of Psychosocial Nursing, Vol.25,* No. 10, 20–24.

Crago, H. (1982) 'The readers in the reader.' *Signal 37, September,* 172–181.

Crago, H. (1983) *Prelude to Literacy.* Southern Illinois University Press.

Cullinan, B. E. and Golda, L. (1981) *Literature and the Child.* Texas, USA: Harcourt Brace.

Darton, F. J. H. (1980) *Children's Books in England.* Cambridge: Cambridge University Press.

De Minco, S. (1995) 'Young adult reaction to death in literature.' New York: *Adolescence, Vol.VI,* 39.

Egoff, S. (ed) (1969) *Only Connect: Readings in Children's Literature.* Canada: Oxford University Press.

Evans, D. (1971) 'Some comments on Robert Tod's article.' London: *Children's Literature in Education:* 46–50.

Fox, G. (ed) (1976) *Writers, Critics and Children.* London: Heinemann.

Fry, D. (1986) *Children Talk About Books.* Milton Keynes: Open University Press.

Harrington, R. (1999) 'Counselling bereaved children may do more harm than good.' London: *Journal of the Royal Society of Medicine, May 1999 issue.*

Haviland, V. (1973) *Children & Literature. Views and Reviews.* London: Bodley Head.

Hollindale, P. (1974) *Choosing Books for Children.* London: Paul Elek.

Hunt, P. (1990) *Children's Literature: The Development of Criticism.* London: Routledge.

Hunt, P. (1991) *Criticism, Theory and Children's Literature.* Oxford: Blackwell.

Hunt, P. (1994) *An Introduction to Children's Literature.* Oxford: Oxford University Press.

Hunt, P. (1995) *Children's Literature: An Illustrated History.* Milton Keynes: Open University Press.

Iser, W. (1974) *The Implied Reader.* Baltimore: Johns Hopkins University Press.

Iser, W. (1978) *The Act of Reading.* Baltimore: Johns Hopkins University Press.

Iser, W. (1989) *Prospecting: From Reader Response to Literary Anthropology.* Baltimore: Johns Hopkins University Press.

Jalongo, M. R. (1983) 'Bibliotherapy: Literature to promote socio-emotional growth.' *Reading Teacher. Volume 36,* 796–803.

Jones, A. and Buttrey, J. (1970) *Children and Stories.* Oxford: Blackwell.

Koubovi, D. (1987) 'Literatherapy: The therapeutic teaching of literature.' London: *Journal of Educational Therapy: Volume 3.*

Landsberg, M. (1988) *The World of Children's Books.* London: Simon & Schuster.

Lenkowsky, R. S (1987) 'Bibliotherapy – a review and analysis of the literature.' *Journal of Special Education 21,* 123–132.

Lesnik-Oberstein, K. (1994) *Children's Literature. Criticism and the Fictional Child.* New York: Oxford University Press.

Marshall, M. R. (1982) *An Introduction to the World of Children's Books.* Aldershot: Gower.

Riordan, R. J. and Wilson, L. S. (1989) 'Bibliotherapy: Does it work?' *Journal of Counselling & Development 67,* 506–507.

Schonfeld, D. J. (1993) 'Talking with children about death.' *Journal of Pediatric Health Care 7,* No. 6, 269–274.

Tod, R. (1971) 'The treatment of childhood stress.' *Children's Literature in Education,* 26–30. London: Ward Lock.

Townsend, J. R. (1965) *Written for Children.* London: Penguin.

Tucker, N. (ed) (1978) *Suitable for Children.* Sussex: Sussex University Press.

Tucker, N. (1981) *The Child and the Book.* Cambridge: Cambridge University Press.

Wall, B. (1991) *The Narrator's Voice.* London: Macmillan.

Walker, M. (1978) 'Last rites for young readers.' *Children's Literature in Education: 1729,* No. 4. 188–197.

Westall, R. (1978) 'How real do you want your realism?' *Signal 28, January,* 34–46.

Whitehead, F., Capey, A. C., Maddern, W. and Wellings, A. (1977) *Children and their Books.* Cambridge: Macmillan.

Wynnejones, P. (1994) 'Beyond this life's outposts.' *Spectrum, 26,* 15–28.

References

Aiken, J. (1965) *Black Hearts in Battersea*. London: Jonathan Cape.

Aiken, J. (1966) *Night Birds in Nantucket*. London: Jonathan Cape.

Aiken, J. (1968) *The Whispering Mountain*. London: Jonathan Cape.

Aiken, J. (1979) *A Touch of Chill*. London: Gollancz.

Aiken, J. (1981) *The Stolen Lake*. London: Jonathan Cape.

Aiken, J. (1986) *Dido and Pa*. London: Jonathan Cape.

Aiken, J. (1987) *A Goose on your Grave*. London: Collins.

Aiken, J. (1993) *A Creepy Company*. London: Gollancz.

Alcott, L. M. (1869) (1965) *Good Wives*. London: Penguin.

Anderson, R. (1996) *Letters from Heaven*. London: Mammoth Books.

Atkinson, E. (1940) (1996) *Greyfriars Bobby*. London: Penguin.

Avery, G. (ed) (1875) (1968) *Froggy's Little Brother*. London: Gollancz.

Baur, M. D. (1987) *On My Honour*. London: Hodder & Stoughton.

Bawden, N. (1994) *The Real Plato Jones*. London: Gollancz.

Bawden, N. (1971) (1982) *Squib*. London: Gollancz.

Bawden, N. (1985) *The Finding*. London: Gollancz.

Blume, J. (1981) *Tiger Eyes*. London: Heinemann.

Branfield, J. (1985) *Fox in Winter*. London: Gollancz.

Brent-Dyer, E. (1929) *Eustacia Goes to the Chalet School*. London: Collins.

Brontë, C. (1847) (1976) *Jane Eyre*. Bristol: Purnell.

Bunting, E. (2000) *Blackwater* London: Collins.

Burnett, F. H. (1905) (1989) *The Little Princess*. London: Warne Lock.

Burnett, F. H. (1911) (1989) *The Secret Garden*. London: Warne Lock.

Burningham, J. (1984) *Granpa*. London: Picture Puffin.

Buscaglia, L. (1982) *The Fall of Freddie the Leaf*. New York: Holt & Rinehart.

Byars, B. (1979) *Goodbye, Chicken Little*. London: Puffin.

Byars, B. (1980) *The Night Swimmers*. London: Puffin.

Carle, E. (1974) *The Very Hungry Caterpillar*. London: Picture Puffin.

Coolidge, S. (1865) *What Katy Did*. London: Blackie.

Cresswell, H. (1988) *The Signposters*. Bath: Chivers.

Dale, E. (1996) *Scrumpy*. London: Anderson Press.

Dalton, A. (1992) *Naming the Dark*. London: Mammoth.

Dean, A. (1992) *Meggie's Magic*. London: Viking.

Dickens, C. (1837) (1984) *Oliver Twist*. London: Cathay Books.

Farrar, F. W. (1858) *Eric or Little by Little*. London: A & C Black.

Fenton, E. (1968) *Horn Book*. Boston: The Horn Book, Inc.

Fitzgerald, S. (1998) *The Tale of Two Dolphins*. Bewdley: Brambles Press.

Fuller, J. (1993) *John's Book*. Cambridge: Lutterworth Press.

Gleitzman, M. (1995) *Two Weeks with the Queen*. London: Macmillan.

Grant, C. (1996) *Shadow Man*. London: Mammoth.

Hamilton, V. (1990) *Cousins*. London: Gollancz.

Hathorn, L. (1994) *Grandma's Shoes*. London: Viking. ·

Herriot, J. (1986) *The Christmas Day Kitten*. London: Michael Joseph.

Hill, D. (1992) *See Ya, Simon*. London: Puffin Penguin.

Hinton, S. E. (1971) *The Outsiders*. London: Gollancz.

Hoy, L. (1981) *Your Friend Rebecca*. London: Bodley Head.

Hunter, M. (1975) *A Sound of Chariots*. London: Fontana.

Johnson, P. (1989) *We, the Haunted*. London: Collins.

Lewis, C. S. (1950) *The Narnia Chronicles*. Oxford: Lion Publishing.

Little, J. (1984) *Mama's Going to Buy You a Mockingbird*. London: Penguin.

Lloyd, C. (1989) *The Charlie Barber Treatment*. London: Walker Books.

Mahy, M. (1995) *Memory*. London: Puffin.

Mansell, D. (1993) *My Old Teddy*. London: Walker Books.

Matthews, A. (1995) *Seeing in Moonlight*. London: Mammoth.

Mayfield, S. (1990) *I Carried You on Eagles' Wings*. London: Scholastic.

Naidoo, B. (2000) *The Other Side of Truth*. London: Puffin.

Newman, M. (1995) *Steve*. London: Watts Books.

Paterson, K. (1977) *Bridge to Terabithia*. London: Penguin.

Rowling, J. K. (1997) *Harry Potter and the Philosopher's Stone*. London: Bloomsbury.

Simmonds, P. (1987) *Fred*. London: Puffin.

Smith, D. B. (1975) *A Taste of Blackberries*. London: Penguin.

Snell, N. (1984) *Emma's Cat Dies*. London: Hamish Hamilton.

Spyri, J. (1880) (1950) *Heidi*. London: J.M. Dent.

Stickney, D. (1984) *Waterbugs and Dragonflies*. London: Mowbray.

Stowe, H. B. (1852) (1982) *Uncle Tom's Cabin*. London: Penguin.

Strachan, I. (1993) *The Boy in the Bubble*. London: Methuen.

Talbert, M. (1988) *Dead Birds Singing*. London: Penguin.

Varley, S. (1984) *Badger's Parting Gifts*. London: Anderson Press.

White, E. B. (1963) *Charlotte's Web*. London: Penguin.

Wilhelm, H. (1985) *I'll Always Love You*. London: Hodder.

Williams, M. (1926) (1995) *The Velveteen Rabbit*. London: Puffin.

Wilson, J. (1989) *Falling Apart*. Oxford: University Press.

Worral, A. (1985) *A Flash of Blue*. London: Methuen.

Purpose-written fictionalised fact

Amos, J. (1990) *Sad*. Bath: Cherrytree Press.

Bryant-Mole, K. (1992) *Death*. Hove: Wayland Press.

Green, W. (1989) *Gran's Grave*. Oxford: Lion.

Haughton, E. (1995) *Dealing With Death*. Hove: Wayland Press.

Hollins, S. and Sireling, L. (1989) *When Mum Died*. Cambridge: Silent Books.

Hollins, S. and Sireling, L. (1989) *When Dad Died*. Cambridge: Silent Books.

Lamont, S. (1989) *Ewen's Little Brother*. Newcastle upon Tyne: Victoria Publications.

Nystrom, C. (1990) *Emma Says Goodbye*. Oxford: Lion Books.

Padoan, G. (1987) *Remembering Grandad*. Swindon: Child's Play International.

Perkins, G. and Morris, L. (1991) *Remembering Mum*. London: Black.

Wadell, M. (1990) *Grandma's Bill*. London: Simon & Schuster.

Subject Index

Name Index